To:

_____

May he turn our hearts to him,
to walk in all his ways.

1 Kings 8:58

From:

_____

Requests for information should be addressed to:
    Inspirio, the Gift Group of Zondervan
    Grand Rapids, Michigan 49530

Senior Editor: Gwen Ellis
Project Editor: Sarah Hupp
Designer: Mark Veldheer

Printed in China

00 01 02 03 04/HK/ 8 7 6 5 4

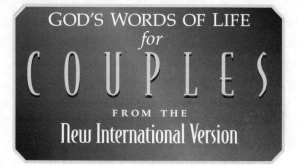

GOD'S WORDS OF LIFE
for
C O U P L E S
FROM THE
New International Version

inspirio
The gift group of Zondervan

Table of Contents

GOD'S WORDS OF LIFE ON

INTRODUCTION
by Les and Leslie Parrott

One of the most compelling love stories of our time involves a couple who in the beginning lived an ocean apart. He was a scruffy old Oxford bachelor, a Christian apologist, and an author of best-selling books for children. She, an American, was much younger and divorced with two sons.

C. S. Lewis met and fell in love with Joy Davidson during a visit she made to England. When she returned home, they fed their relationship by mail. Then when Joy moved to England with her boys, the relationship flourished. After a time, her departure from England seemed imminent because of a lack of funds and an expiring visitor's visa. C. S. Lewis made a decision: If Joy would agree, they would be married.

He said of their relationship: "We feasted on love; every mode of it, solemn and merry, romantic and realistic, sometimes as dramatic as a thunderstorm, sometimes comfortable and unemphatic as putting on your soft slippers."

Early in their marriage, Joy's body revealed a secret—she had cancer. The well-ordered life of C. S. Lewis suffered a meltdown as he realized how deep his love for Joy really was.

Lewis gave Joy the best treatment available. Then he brought her home and committed himself to her care. It is not surprising that Joy's body responded. However, her remission was short-lived and the cancer became terminal.

Near death, Joy told him, "You have made me happy." Then, a little while after she added, "I am at peace with God."

If there is a lesson to be gained from this tender love story, it must be that partners without a spiritual depth of oneness can never compete with the fullness of love that soul mates enjoy. Marriage, when it is healthy, has a mystical way of revealing God; a way of bringing a smiling peace to our restless hearts.

When researchers examined the characteristics of happy couples who had been married for more than two decades, one of the most important qualities they found was "faith in God and spiritual commitment."

God loves marriage enough to make it a picture of his relationship to the church, and his Word, the Bible, is a love letter to his bride. We can learn much about how we should relate to one another within our marriage relationships as we read about God's relationship to his bride. *God's Words of Life for Couples* is a devotional book that will encourage each of you individually and also as a couple. Enjoy your time together as you read, meditate upon, and discuss *God's Words of Life for Couples*.

God's Words of Life *on*
ACCEPTANCE

Do to others as you would have them do to you.

Luke 6:31

To love him with all your heart, with all your understanding and with all your strength, and to love your neighbor as yourself is more important than all burnt offerings and sacrifices.

Mark 12:33

I have set you an example that you should do as I have done for you.

John 13:15

He who receives you receives me, and he who receives me receives the one who sent me.

Matthew 10:40

How good and pleasant it is when brothers live together in unity!

Psalm 133:1

Give to the one who asks you, and do not turn away from the one who wants to borrow from you. You have heard that it was said, "Love your neighbor and hate your enemy." But I tell you: Love your enemies and pray for those who persecute you.

Matthew 5:42–44

ACCEPTANCE

My command is this: Love each other as I have loved you. Greater love has no one than this, that he lay down his life for his friends.

John 15:12–13

Be devoted to one another in brotherly love. Honor one another above yourselves.

Romans 12:10

May the LORD make your love increase and overflow for each other and for everyone else, just as ours does for you.

1 Thessalonians 3:12

Let us consider how we may spur one another on toward love and good deeds.

Hebrews 10:24

If you really keep the royal law found in Scripture, "Love your neighbor as yourself," you are doing right.

James 2:8

Above all, love each other deeply, because love covers over a multitude of sins.

1 Peter 4:8

Dear friends, let us love one another, for love comes from God. Everyone who loves has been born of God and knows God.

1 John 4:7

God's Words of Life on
ACCEPTANCE

He himself is our peace, who has made the two one and has destroyed the barrier, the dividing wall of hostility.

Ephesians 2:14

The body is a unit, though it is made up of many parts; and though all its parts are many, they form one body. So it is with Christ.

1 Corinthians 12:12

There is neither Jew nor Greek, slave nor free, male nor female, for you are all one in Christ Jesus.

Galatians 3:28

Make room for us in your hearts.

2 Corinthians 7:2

God has shown me that I should not call any man impure or unclean.

Acts 10:28

God's Words of Life on
ACCEPTANCE

ACCEPT THE DIFFERENCES

People tend to focus on what's wrong with the world rather than what's right, and that trickles over into our relationships. Instead of being like diamond miners who sift through the dirt looking for one gem, we sift through all the diamonds looking for a little dirt.

Most couples don't start out focusing on their partner's negative traits. When people are dating, they often say things like, "We're so much alike." But once they get married, their differences become more apparent. Whenever couples fall into judging each other's actions against personal codes of behavior, they need to understand one important truth: Differences are just differences. There is no right or wrong when it comes to personalities.

In contrast, affirming your partner's strengths goes a long way toward creating an uplifting atmosphere. Don't assume your spouse knows what his or her strengths are; point them out. The more you can express appreciation, the stronger your relationship will be. By focusing on the positives, you will be reminded just why you married the person you did.

Preston and Genie Dyer

God's Words of Life *on*
ANGER

Do not be quickly provoked in your spirit, for anger resides in the lap of fools.

Ecclesiastes 7:9

Take note of this: Everyone should be quick to listen, slow to speak and slow to become angry, for man's anger does not bring about the righteous life that God desires.

James 1:19–20

A patient man has great understanding, but a quick-tempered man displays folly.

Proverbs 14:29

"In your anger do not sin": Do not let the sun go down while you are still angry, and do not give the devil a foothold.

Ephesians 4:26–27

A gentle answer turns away wrath, but a harsh word stirs up anger.

Proverbs 15:1

Do not take revenge, my friends, but leave room for God's wrath, for it is written: "It is mine to avenge; I will repay," says the Lord. On the contrary: "If your enemy is hungry, feed him; if he is thirsty, give him something to drink. In doing this, you will heap burning

coals on his head." Do not be overcome by
evil, but overcome evil with good.

Romans 12:19–21

For we know him who said, "It is mine to
avenge; I will repay," and again, "The Lord
will judge his people."

Hebrews 10:30

Better a patient man than a warrior, a man who
controls his temper than one who takes a city.

Proverbs 16:32

Get rid of all bitterness, rage and anger,
brawling and slander, along with every form
of malice. Be kind and compassionate to one
another, forgiving each other, just as in Christ
God forgave you.

Ephesians 4:31–32

A wise man fears the LORD and shuns evil,
but a fool is hotheaded and reckless. A quick-
tempered man does foolish things, and a
crafty man is hated.

Proverbs 14:16–17

A hot-tempered man stirs up dissension, but
a patient man calms a quarrel.

Proverbs 15:18

God's Words of Life on
ANGER

Starting a quarrel is like breaching a dam; so drop the matter before a dispute breaks out.

Proverbs 17:14

Do not make friends with a hot-tempered man, do not associate with one easily angered, or you may learn his ways and get yourself ensnared.

Proverbs 22:24–25

I want men everywhere to lift up holy hands in prayer, without anger or disputing.

1 Timothy 2:8

Why are you angry? Why is your face downcast? If you do what is right, will you not be accepted? But if you do not do what is right, sin is crouching at your door; it desires to have you, but you must master it.

Genesis 4:6–7

Refrain from anger and turn from wrath; do not fret—it leads only to evil.

Psalm 37:8

CONTROLLING ANGER

It's not anger itself that has moral implications—it's how you handle it. The good news is that either one of you can decide to change the established patterns. Learning to discharge your anger in non-destructive ways brings life and vitality to your marriage.

First, express your own feelings rather than hurling blame or launching a character assassination against your mate.

Second, use preambles for introducing heavy topics. Melissa and I often say, "This is not something you need to 'fix,' I just need to talk out some feelings." That gives the other person a chance to begin listening in a focused, non-defensive way.

Third, increase your "critical interval"—the time between a stimulus and a response. The old advice of counting to ten is a good way to begin dealing with a short temper. Simply delay your response until your objectivity has returned.

Finally, and most important: Kiss and make up. When the dust settles and you've heard each other out, get forgiveness into the picture. And when forgiving one another is difficult, stop to consider the alternative. Prolonged loneliness and lingering bitterness are simply not worth it.

Louis McBurney, M.D.

God's Words of Life *on*
CHANGE

I the LORD do not change.

Malachi 3:6

The Father of the heavenly lights ... does not change like shifting shadows.

James 1:17

He who is the Glory of Israel does not lie or change his mind; for he is not a man, that he should change his mind.

1 Samuel 15:29

You were taught, with regard to your former way of life, to put off your old self, which is being corrupted by its deceitful desires; to be made new in the attitude of your minds; and to put on the new self, created to be like God in true righteousness and holiness.

Ephesians 4:22–24

If anyone is in Christ, he is a new creation; the old has gone, the new has come!

2 Corinthians 5:17

By dying to what once bound us, we have been released from the law so that we serve in the new way of the Spirit, and not in the old way of the written code.

Romans 7:6

Since, then, you have been raised with Christ,
set your hearts on things above, where Christ
is seated at the right hand of God. Set your
minds on things above, not on earthly things.
For you died, and your life is now hidden
with Christ in God.

Colossians 3:1–3

Jesus Christ is the same yesterday and today
and forever.

Hebrews 13:8

You, however, are controlled not by the sinful
nature but by the Spirit, if the Spirit of God
lives in you.

Romans 8:9

When I was a child, I talked like a child, I
thought like a child, I reasoned like a child.
When I became a man, I put childish ways
behind me.

1 Corinthians 13:11

We know that our old self was crucified with
him so that the body of sin might be done
away with, that we should no longer be
slaves to sin—because anyone who has died
has been freed from sin.

Romans 6:6–7

God's Words of Life *on*
CHANGE

Behold, I will create new heavens and a new earth. The former things will not be remembered, nor will they come to mind. But be glad and rejoice forever in what I will create.

Isaiah 65:17–18

Forget the former things; do not dwell on the past. See, I am doing a new thing! Now it springs up; do you not perceive it? I am making a way in the desert and streams in the wasteland.

Isaiah 43:18–19

THE MOUNTAIN OF CHANGE

Some changes come with time: passions cool, energies wane and children and careers intrude on the amount of time a couple can spend together. Other changes occur by design, as happens when a couple sets out to alter each other's behavior.

Usually, one spouse's attempts to change the other end in failure. However, two people can make each other more compatible through "mutual education." Each partner helps change the other by seeking to replace one behavior with another that is more preferable. And always at the heart of mutual education is the principle of gentle persuasion, not coerced change. Any effort to help your spouse change should send the message: "I love you. I believe this change would benefit you and it will mean much to me. Would you give it a try?"

Affirm the value of change, and remember that it's a two-way street. The two of you are like mountain climbers, each lending a hand to the other, making suggestions and giving encouragement, as you work toward the same goal: a stronger, more fulfilling relationship.

Jeanette and Robert Lauer

God's Words of Life *on*
COMMITMENT

Christ's command is this: Love each other as I have loved you.

John 15:12

Let love and faithfulness never leave you; bind them around your neck, write them on the tablet of your heart.

Proverbs 3:3

It is required that those who have been given a trust must prove faithful.

1 Corinthians 4:2

You were called to be free. But do not use your freedom to indulge the sinful nature; rather, serve one another in love.

Galatians 5:13

Love one another deeply, from the heart.

1 Peter 1:22

May the God who gives endurance and encouragement give you a spirit of unity among yourselves as you follow Christ Jesus.

Romans 15:5

Be completely humble and gentle; be patient, bearing with one another in love.

Ephesians 4:2

Bear with each other and forgive whatever grievances you may have against one another. Forgive as the Lord forgave you. And over all these virtues put on love, which binds them all together in perfect unity.

Colossians 3:13–14

Be kind and compassionate to one another.

Ephesians 4:32

In everything, do to others what you would have them do to you.

Matthew 7:12

It was said to the people long ago, "Do not break your oath, but keep the oaths you have made to the Lord."

Matthew 5:33

Honor one another above yourselves.

Romans 12:10

Live a life of love, just as Christ loved us and gave himself up for us as a fragrant offering and sacrifice to God.

Ephesians 5:2

You yourselves have been taught by God to love each other.

1 Thessalonians 4:9

God's Words of Life *on*
COMMITMENT

Love is patient, love is kind. It does not envy, it does not boast, it is not proud. It is not rude, it is not self-seeking, it is not easily angered, it keeps no record of wrongs. Love does not delight in evil but rejoices with the truth.

1 Corinthians 13:4–6

May the Lord make your love increase and overflow for each other.

1 Thessalonians 3:12

I will give them singleness of heart and action, so that they will always fear me for their own good and the good of their children after them.

Jeremiah 32:39

The only thing that counts is faith expressing itself through love.

Galatians 5:6

A faithful man will be richly blessed.

Proverbs 28:20

Your hearts must be fully committed to the Lord our God, to live by his decrees and obey his commands.

1 Kings 8:61

COMMITMENT

Commit your way to the LORD; trust in him and he will do this: He will make your righteousness shine like the dawn.

Psalm 37:5–6

Commit to the LORD whatever you do, and your plans will succeed.

Proverbs 16:3

I press on toward the goal to win the prize for which God has called me heavenward in Christ Jesus.

Philippians 3:14

Each one should use whatever gift he has received to serve others, faithfully administering God's grace in its various forms.

1 Peter 4:10

Let us not become weary in doing good, for at the proper time we will reap a harvest if we do not give up.

Galatians 6:9

Be strong and do not give up, for your work will be rewarded.

2 Chronicles 15:7

Serve wholeheartedly.

Ephesians 6:7

God's Words of Life *on*
COMMITMENT

Be devoted to one another in . . . love.

Romans 12:10

Marriage should be honored by all.

Hebrews 13:4

It is required that those who have been given a trust must prove faithful.

1 Corinthians 4:2

Place me like a seal over your heart, like a seal on your arm.

Song of Songs 8:6

I belong to my lover, and his desire is for me.

Song of Songs 7:10

STICKING IT OUT

There is woven into the fabric of marriage a sense of something ongoing. One woman, one man, together for a lifetime. They don't have to be "communicating" or having fun or constantly setting goals. They do have to be together—and intend to stay that way. This is faithfulness to each other and to God.

Too many people think marriage should be fun, or fulfilling, or entertaining. Then they get married and find out it's not always like that. So they keep searching and find even more frustration with another marriage partner.

As I read Scripture, I don't see teachings on happiness as a first principle. Joy, yes—the kind of joy that flows from obedience, from service, from glimpses of the holy. God wants us to do that which glorifies him—to be faithful, to keep his commandments, to seek first his Kingdom. Sticking it out comes first in God's eyes.

Sticking it out means being faithful, and out of faithfulness there is peace. I see that peace in couples who have been married years and years. These are the couples who have come to terms with their choices, they accept each other wholly, and somewhere along the line they embraced sticking it out as a first principle.

Elizabeth Cody Newenhuyse

God's Words of Life *on*
COMMUNICATION

A man finds joy in giving an apt reply—and how good is a timely word!

Proverbs 15:23

The Sovereign LORD has given me an instructed tongue, to know the word that sustains the weary. He wakens me morning by morning, wakens my ear to listen like one being taught.

Isaiah 50:4

From the fruit of his lips a man is filled with good things as surely as the work of his hands rewards him.

Proverbs 12:14

You must rid yourselves of all such things as these: anger, rage, malice, slander, and filthy language from your lips. Do not lie to each other, since you have taken off your old self with its practices.

Colossians 3:8–9

Do not let any unwholesome talk come out of your mouths, but only what is helpful for building others up according to their needs, that it may benefit those who listen.

Ephesians 4:29

COMMUNICATION

Let your conversation be always full of grace,
seasoned with salt, so that you may know
how to answer everyone.

Colossians 4:6

Out of the overflow of the heart the mouth
speaks.

Matthew 12:34

An honest answer is like a kiss on the lips.

Proverbs 24:26

Do everything without complaining or arguing.

Philippians 2:14

We all stumble in many ways. If anyone is
never at fault in what he says, he is a perfect
man, able to keep his whole body in check.
When we put bits into the mouths of horses
to make them obey us, we can turn the whole
animal...Likewise the tongue is a small part
of the body, but it makes great boasts.
Consider what a great forest is set on fire by
a small spark. The tongue also is a fire, a
world of evil among the parts of the body. It
corrupts the whole person, sets the whole
course of his life on fire, and is itself set on
fire by hell . . . No man can tame the tongue.
It is a restless evil, full of deadly poison.

James 3:2–8

God's Words of Life *on*
COMMUNICATION

Keep your tongue from evil and your lips from speaking lies. Turn from evil and do good; seek peace and pursue it.

Psalm 34:13–14

Words from a wise man's mouth are gracious, but a fool is consumed by his own lips. At the beginning his words are folly; at the end they are wicked madness—and the fool multiplies words.

Ecclesiastes 10:12–13

He who guards his lips guards his life, but he who speaks rashly will come to ruin.

Proverbs 13:3

Whoever would love life and see good days must keep his tongue from evil and his lips from deceitful speech.

1 Peter 3:10

The tongue has the power of life and death, and those who love it will eat its fruit.

Proverbs 18:21

The tongue of the righteous is choice silver, but the heart of the wicked is of little value.

Proverbs 10:20

Speaking the truth in love, we will in all things grow up into him who is the Head, that is, Christ.

Ephesians 4:15

A word aptly spoken is like apples of gold in settings of silver.

Proverbs 25:11

My words come from an upright heart; my lips sincerely speak what I know.

Job 33:3

The mouth of the righteous man utters wisdom, and his tongue speaks what is just.

Psalm 37:30

I will watch my ways and keep my tongue from sin; I will put a muzzle on my mouth.

Psalm 39:1

A gossip betrays a confidence, but a trustworthy man keeps a secret.

Proverbs 11:13

Reckless words pierce like a sword, but the tongue of the wise brings healing.

Proverbs 12:18

God's Words of Life on
COMMUNICATION

A fool finds no pleasure in understanding but delights in airing his own opinions.

Proverbs 18:2

She speaks with wisdom, and faithful instruction is on her tongue. A woman who fears the LORD is to be praised.

Proverbs 31:26–30

May the words of my mouth and the meditation of my heart be pleasing in your sight, O LORD, my Rock and my Redeemer.

Psalm 19:14

The lips of the righteous know what is fitting.

Proverbs 10:32

The heart of the righteous weighs its answers.

Proverbs 15:28

Do not repay evil with evil or insult with insult, but with blessing, because to this you were called so that you may inherit a blessing.

1 Peter 3:9

COMMUNICATION MEANS CARING

Communication between a woman and a man is very different from what happens when two women talk. When two women get together, they do a lot of explaining and restating until the other person understands what is being said.

But a man may say something vague, such as, "I don't know. I guess my job is really tough." After making that short statement, he may drop it. His wife assumes it must not be a big problem since he didn't say more than two sentences. But she needs to pick up on the little phrase that he did say. He's feeling a great loss, but he's not expressing it. Women need to listen to the small phrases that their husbands are saying and then respond accordingly.

A man needs a wife who cares enough to listen to the brief, sometimes weak, signals that he gives off. And then respond with gentle questions to draw him out, not by taking the opportunity to describe her own struggles. When one spouse is drawn away by someone outside the marriage, it's usually not that he's being drawn away by love. More often, he is drawn away because someone else showed they cared.

Jim and Sally Conway

God's Words of Life on
CONFLICT

A prudent man overlooks an insult.

Proverbs 12:16

A gentle answer turns away wrath, but a harsh word stirs up anger.

Proverbs 15:1

Do not be quickly provoked in your spirit, for anger resides in the lap of fools.

Ecclesiastes 7:9

Whatever happens, conduct yourselves in a manner worthy of the gospel of Christ.

Philippians 1:27

If anyone says, "I love God," yet hates his brother, he is a liar. For anyone who does not love his brother, whom he has seen, cannot love God, whom he has not seen. And he has given us this command: Whoever loves God must also love his brother.

1 John 4:20–21

Love is patient, love is kind. It does not envy, it does not boast, it is not proud. It is not rude, it is not self-seeking, it is not easily angered, it keeps no record of wrongs.

1 Corinthians 13:4–5

Do not be overcome by evil, but overcome
evil with good.

Romans 12:21

May the God who gives endurance and
encouragement give you a spirit of unity
among yourselves as you follow Christ Jesus,
so that with one heart and mouth you may
glorify the God and Father of our Lord Jesus
Christ. Accept one another, then, just as
Christ accepted you, in order to bring praise
to God.

Romans 15:5–7

I appeal to you, brothers, in the name of our
Lord Jesus Christ, that all of you agree with
one another so that there may be no divisions
among you and that you may be perfectly
united in mind and thought.

1 Corinthians 1:10

Make my joy complete by being like-minded,
having the same love, being one in spirit and
purpose. Do nothing out of selfish ambition
or vain conceit, but in humility consider
others better than yourselves. Each of you
should look not only to your own interests,
but also to the interests of others.

Philippians 2:2–4

God's Words of Life *on*
CONFLICT

Let us therefore make every effort to do what leads to peace and to mutual edification.

Romans 14:19

Refrain from anger and turn from wrath; do not fret—it leads only to evil.

Psalm 37:8

A hot-tempered man stirs up dissension, but a patient man calms a quarrel.

Proverbs 15:18

Starting a quarrel is like breaching a dam; so drop the matter before a dispute breaks out.

Proverbs 17:14

A man's wisdom gives him patience; it is to his glory to overlook an offense.

Proverbs 19:11

Do not make friends with a hot-tempered man, do not associate with one easily angered, or you may learn his ways and get yourself ensnared.

Proverbs 22:24–25

Hatred stirs up dissension, but love covers over all wrongs.

Proverbs 10:12

Be kind and compassionate to one another, forgiving each other, just as in Christ God forgave you.

Ephesians 4:32

"In your anger do not sin": Do not let the sun go down while you are still angry, and do not give the devil a foothold.

Ephesians 4:26–27

I want men everywhere to lift up holy hands in prayer, without anger or disputing.

1 Timothy 2:8

Take note of this: Everyone should be quick to listen, slow to speak and slow to become angry, for man's anger does not bring about the righteous life that God desires.

James 1:19–20

Finally, all of you, live in harmony with one another; be sympathetic, love as brothers, be compassionate and humble. Do not repay evil with evil or insult with insult, but with blessing, because to this you were called so that you may inherit a blessing.

1 Peter 3:8–9

How good and pleasant it is when brothers live together in unity!

Psalm 133:1

God's Words of Life on
CONFLICT

In your anger do not sin; when you are on your beds, search your hearts and be silent.

Psalm 4:4

The tongue that brings healing is a tree of life, but a deceitful tongue crushes the spirit.

Proverbs 15:4

He who pursues righteousness and love finds life, prosperity and honor.

Proverbs 21:21

A fool gives full vent to his anger, but a wise man keeps himself under control.

Proverbs 29:11

Do not be quickly provoked in your spirit.

Ecclesiastes 7:9

A patient man has great understanding, but a quick-tempered man displays folly.

Proverbs 14:29

Pride only breeds quarrels, but wisdom is found in those who take advice.

Proverbs 13:10

LEARN TO FIGHT CLEAN

Most marriages have their periodic skirmishes—and, occasionally, an all-out war. We can't stamp out fighting completely, but we can learn how to fight clean. Here are Biblical ground rules for marital battles.

First, commit yourselves to honesty and mutual respect. Have you committed yourself, verbally and honestly in your soul, to being authentic and honest with your partner, viewing him or her with respect?

Next, lay down your deadly weapons. A temper that slips out of control is sinful. Anger that means to hurt is sin.

Third, agree with your mate that the time is right. Both partners should sense when to talk. There are times to disagree, and there are times not to disagree.

Fourth, after you take a verbal swing, be ready with a solution. When you come to your mate with justified criticism, be quick with a suggested solution.

Fifth, watch your words and guard your tone. The louder our voices, the less our mate will hear; the uglier the words, the less we all communicate.

Finally, when it's all over, help clean up the mess. Be compassionate enough to weep with the one who's hurt from the fight.

Charles R. Swindoll

God's Words of Life on
COURAGE

The LORD is my light and my salvation—
whom shall I fear? The LORD is the stronghold of my life—of whom shall I be afraid?

Psalm 27:1

Do not fear, for I am with you; do not be dismayed, for I am your God. I will strengthen
you and help you; I will uphold you with my
righteous right hand.

Isaiah 41:10

I can do everything through him who gives
me strength.

Philippians 4:13

Do not be surprised at the painful trial you
are suffering, as though something strange
were happening to you. But rejoice that you
participate in the sufferings of Christ, so that
you may be overjoyed when his glory is
revealed.

1 Peter 4:12–13

When you pass through the waters, I will be
with you; and when you pass through the
rivers, they will not sweep over you. When
you walk through the fire, you will not be
burned; the flames will not set you ablaze.

Isaiah 43:2

God's Words of Life *on*
COURAGE

We are more than conquerors through him who loved us. For I am convinced that neither death nor life, neither angels nor demons, neither the present nor the future, nor any powers, neither height nor depth, nor anything else in all creation, will be able to separate us from the love of God that is in Christ Jesus our Lord.

Romans 8:37–39

Be strong and take heart, all you who hope in the LORD.

Psalm 31:24

Be strong and courageous. Do not be terrified; do not be discouraged, for the LORD your God will be with you wherever you go.

Joshua 1:9

He gives strength to the weary and increases the power of the weak. Even youths grow tired and weary, and young men stumble and fall; but those who hope in the LORD will renew their strength. They will soar on wings like eagles; they will run and not grow weary, they will walk and not be faint.

Isaiah 40:29–31

Wait for the LORD; be strong and take heart and wait for the LORD.

Psalm 27:14

God's Words of Life on
COURAGE

Strengthen the feeble hands, steady the knees that give way; say to those with fearful hearts, "Be strong, do not fear; your God will come, he will come with vengeance."

Isaiah 35:3–4

Be strong and very courageous. Be careful to obey all the law my servant Moses gave you; do not turn from it to the right or to the left, that you may be successful wherever you go.

Joshua 1:7

Observe what the LORD your God requires . . . so that you may prosper in all you do and wherever you go.

1 Kings 2:2–3

Do not be anxious about anything, but in everything, by prayer and petition, with thanksgiving, present your requests to God. And the peace of God, which transcends all understanding, will guard your hearts and your minds in Christ Jesus. Finally, brothers, whatever is true, whatever is noble, whatever is right, whatever is pure, whatever is lovely, whatever is admirable—if anything is excellent or praiseworthy—think about such things.

Philippians 4:6–8

God's Words of Life *on*
COURAGE

Be strong and courageous. Do not be afraid
or discouraged because of the king of Assyria
and the vast army with him, for there is a
greater power with us than with him. With
him is only the arm of flesh, but with us is
the LORD our God to help us and to fight our
battles.

2 Chronicles 32:7–8

He said. "Peace! Be strong now; be strong."
When he spoke to me, I was strengthened
and said, "Speak, my Lord, since you have
given me strength."

Daniel 10:19

Be strong in the Lord and in his mighty
power.

Ephesians 6:10

Strengthen your feeble arms and weak knees.
"Make level paths for your feet," so that the
lame may not be disabled, but rather healed.

Hebrews 12:12–13

God's Words of Life on
COURAGE

Act with courage, and may the LORD be with those who do well.

2 Chronicles 19:11

During the fourth watch of the night Jesus went out to them, walking on the lake. When the disciples saw him walking on the lake, they were terrified. "It's a ghost," they said, and cried out in fear. But Jesus immediately said to them: "Take courage! It is I. Don't be afraid."

Matthew 14:25–27

Be on your guard; stand firm in the faith; be men of courage; be strong. Do everything in love.

1 Corinthians 16:13–14

Do not be afraid... I am your shield, your very great reward.

Genesis 15:1

In God, whose word I praise, in God I trust; I will not be afraid. What can mortal man do to me?

Psalm 56:4

Surely God is my salvation; I will trust and not be afraid.

Isaiah 12:2

HAVE COURAGE ENOUGH TO RISK

My natural bent is toward the safe way. If I have a choice, I will not drive unknown mountain roads in the fog or walk the neighborhood after dark. And I often find myself choosing the low-risk way in other areas. I would rather swim laps at the neighborhood pool than join my husband for a game of tennis because I know I can "win" at swimming laps by myself.

But I am convinced that, as a child of God, I am called to risk. Christ's invitation to risk comes to me even as it came to his disciple, Peter, one dark and windy night on Lake Gennesaret.

"Come," Jesus called. The command seemed illogical and contained no guarantee of safety or reward. But Peter obeyed and ventured out onto the surface of the water. We do not think of Peter's risk as highly successful. "You of little faith... why did you doubt?" (Matthew 14:31) Jesus chided after Peter's near-drowning. But Peter had taken a risk. Years later he would stand before a hostile crowd and declare, "There is no other name... by which we must be saved" (Acts 4:12). His audience marveled at his courage—courage that perhaps began to grow on a dark and windy night at sea. Without risk there is no opportunity for personal growth.

Ruth Senter 43

God's Words of Life *on*
DECISION-MAKING

The heart of the discerning acquires knowledge; the ears of the wise seek it out.

Proverbs 18:15

If any of you lacks wisdom, he should ask God, who gives generously to all without finding fault, and it will be given to him.

James 1:5

Give your servant a discerning heart to govern your people and to distinguish between right and wrong.

1 Kings 3:9

The discerning heart seeks knowledge.

Proverbs 15:14

Wise men store up knowledge.

Proverbs 10:14

This is the confidence we have in approaching God: that if we ask anything according to his will, he hears us.

1 John 5:14

Your commands make me wiser than my enemies, for they are ever with me. I have more insight than all my teachers, for I meditate on your statutes. I have more understanding than the elders, for I obey your precepts.

Psalm 119:98–100

God's Words of Life *on*
DECISION-MAKING

Instruct a wise man and he will be wiser still; teach a righteous man and he will add to his learning.

Proverbs 9:9

Get wisdom, get understanding; do not forget my words or swerve from them. Do not forsake wisdom, and she will protect you; love her, and she will watch over you. Wisdom is supreme; therefore get wisdom. Though it cost all you have, get understanding.

Proverbs 4:5–7

The way of a fool seems right to him, but a wise man listens to advice.

Proverbs 12:15

Show me your ways, O LORD, teach me your paths; guide me in your truth and teach me, for you are God my Savior, and my hope is in you all day long.

Psalm 25:4–5

Trust in the LORD with all your heart and lean not on your own understanding; in all your ways acknowledge him, and he will make your paths straight.

Proverbs 3:5–6

God's Words of Life on
DECISION-MAKING

Your word is a lamp to my feet and a light
for my path.

Psalm 119:105

Let the wise listen and add to their learning,
and let the discerning get guidance.

Proverbs 1:5

Make plans by seeking advice.

Proverbs 20:18

Since you are my rock and my fortress, for
the sake of your name lead and guide me.

Psalm 31:3

Send forth your light and your truth, let them
guide me.

Psalm 43:3

The LORD will guide you always; he will satisfy your needs in a sun-scorched land and
will strengthen your frame. You will be like a
well-watered garden, like a spring whose
waters never fail.

Isaiah 58:11

GUIDELINES FOR GOOD DECISIONS

The next time you and your spouse face a major decision, answer yes or no to each question below before settling on a course of action.

1. Is the contemplated action in accordance with the Ten Commandments? Is it consistent with Jesus' commandment to "love one another as I have loved you"?
2. Is it something we would want everyone to know about?
3. Five or ten years from now, will both of us be pleased to have done this?
4. Is it something Jesus would do?
5. Will either of us feel regret or gratitude after the deed is done? If it is left undone?
6. Have we prayed about this decision?
7. Would this be hurtful to either one of us, to our marriage or to others? Would it be helpful to either one of us, to our marriage or to others?

Lowell and Carol Erdahl

God's Words of Life *on*
ENCOURAGEMENT

You are a gracious and merciful God.

Nehemiah 9:31

You, O LORD, are a compassionate and gracious God, slow to anger, abounding in love and faithfulness.

Psalm 86:15

Who is a God like you, who pardons sin? You do not stay angry forever but delight to show mercy. You will again have compassion on us; you will tread our sins underfoot and hurl all our iniquities into the depths of the sea.

Micah 7:18–19

Though I have fallen, I will rise. Though I sit in darkness, the LORD will be my light.

Micah 7:8

His mercy extends to those who fear him, from generation to generation.

Luke 1:50

This I call to mind and therefore I have hope: Because of the LORD's great love we are not consumed, for his compassions never fail. They are new every morning; great is your faithfulness.

Lamentations 3:21–23

He who trusts in himself is a fool, but he who walks in wisdom is kept safe.

Proverbs 28:26

God, who has called you into fellowship with his Son Jesus Christ our Lord, is faithful.

1 Corinthians 1:9

Commit to the LORD whatever you do, and your plans will succeed.

Proverbs 16:3

The LORD is good to those whose hope is in him, to the one who seeks him.

Lamentations 3:25

May the God who gives endurance and encouragement give you a spirit of unity among yourselves as you follow Christ Jesus, so that with one heart and mouth you may glorify the God and Father of our Lord Jesus Christ.

Romans 15:5–6

An anxious heart weighs a man down, but a kind word cheers him up.

Proverbs 12:25

My mouth would encourage you; comfort from my lips would bring you relief.

Job 16:5

49

God's Words of Life on
ENCOURAGEMENT

If you have any encouragement from being united with Christ, if any comfort from his love, if any fellowship with the Spirit, if any tenderness and compassion, then make my joy complete by being like-minded, having the same love, being one in spirit and purpose. Do nothing out of selfish ambition or vain conceit, but in humility consider others better than yourselves. Each of you should look not only to your own interests, but also to the interests of others.

Philippians 2:1–4

May our Lord Jesus Christ himself and God our Father, who loved us and by his grace gave us eternal encouragement and good hope, encourage your hearts and strengthen you in every good deed and word.

2 Thessalonians 2:16–17

Your love has given me great joy and encouragement.

Philemon 1:7

TALENT SCOUTS NEEDED

Each of us needs encouragement, especially from our spouse. But how can we best tell our partner "I believe in you"? A good place to start is by encouraging, giving the benefit of the doubt and thinking the best of your mate.

It's easy to be a critic, but it's much more rewarding to be an encourager. When you criticize, you are standing against your spouse. When you encourage, however, you stand beside him or her. The Hebrew term for encourage conveys the idea of putting strength into someone's hands, arms or body so they can handle pressure.

In order to do a better job of encouraging, you need to become a "talent scout" by seeking out your mate's underdeveloped potential. Most of us have been conditioned instead to look for people's liabilities. Perhaps this approach makes us feel better about our own imperfections, but it's not very pleasant to live in such an environment.

Encouragement means not taking your partner for granted. Your spouse is a unique gift to you, and he or she needs constant recognition. Too many people suffer from emotional malnutrition because they are receiving too little encouragement.

H. Norman Wright

God's Words of Life *on* FAITH

Build yourselves up in your most holy faith and pray in the Holy Spirit.

Jude 1:20

Therefore, since we have been justified through faith we have peace with God through our Lord Jesus Christ.

Romans 5:1

Have faith in the LORD your God and you will be upheld.

2 Chronicles 20:20

Make every effort to add to your faith goodness; and to goodness, knowledge; and to knowledge, self-control; and to self-control, perseverance; and to perseverance, godliness; and to godliness, brotherly kindness; and to brotherly kindness, love. For if you possess these qualities in increasing measure, they will keep you from being ineffective and unproductive in your knowledge of our Lord Jesus Christ.

2 Peter 1:5–8

Faith comes from hearing the message, and the message is heard through the word of Christ.

Romans 10:17

Let us fix our eyes on Jesus, the author and perfecter of our faith, who for the joy set before him endured the cross, scorning its shame, and sat down at the right hand of the throne of God.

Hebrews 12:2

Abram believed the LORD, and he credited it to him as righteousness.

Genesis 15:6

Faith is being sure of what we hope for and certain of what we do not see.

Hebrews 11:1

Jesus said: "I tell you the truth, if you have faith as small as a mustard seed, you can say to this mountain, 'Move from here to there' and it will move. Nothing will be impossible for you."

Matthew 17:20

We live by faith, not by sight.

2 Corinthians 5:7

God's Words of Life on
FAITH

In the gospel a righteousness from God is revealed, a righteousness that is by faith from first to last, just as it is written: "The righteous will live by faith."

Romans 1:17

These have come so that your faith—of greater worth than gold, which perishes even though refined by fire—may be proved genuine and may result in praise, glory and honor when Jesus Christ is revealed. Though you have not seen him, you love him; and even though you do not see him now, you believe in him and are filled with an inexpressible and glorious joy, for you are receiving the goal of your faith, the salvation of your souls.

1 Peter 1:7–9

A woman who had been subject to bleeding for twelve years came up behind him and touched the edge of his cloak. She said to herself, "If I only touch his cloak, I will be healed." Jesus turned and saw her. "Take heart, daughter," he said, "your faith has healed you." And the woman was healed from that moment.

Matthew 9:20–22

Jesus said: "I tell you the truth, if anyone says to this mountain, 'Go, throw yourself into the sea,' and does not doubt in his heart but believes that what he says will happen, it will be done for him. Therefore I tell you, whatever you ask for in prayer, believe that you have received it, and it will be yours."

Mark 11:22–24

Faith comes from hearing the message, and the message is heard through the word of Christ.

Romans 10:17

If I have a faith that can move mountains, but have not love, I am nothing.

1 Corinthians 13:2

[Jesus] touched their eyes and said, "According to your faith will it be done to you."

Matthew 9:29

Without faith it is impossible to please God, because anyone who comes to him must believe that he exists and that he rewards those who earnestly seek him.

Hebrews 11:6

God's Words of Life on
FAITH

This is the victory that has overcome the world, even our faith.

1 John 5:4

Be on your guard; stand firm in the faith; be men of courage; be strong. Do everything in love.

1 Corinthians 16:13–14

MYSTERY OF FAITH

I know a 76-year-old woman whose husband died after fifty-four years of marriage. Sam had been sick for two years before he died, and his wife was beside him the whole time. In the end, he couldn't speak, so he wasn't able to say good-bye to her. She grieved over that. But God comforted her, she said, by showing her that everything that needed to be spoken had been said over their fifty-four years together.

"Somehow," she told me, "God takes the awfulness out of each experience and sets you on your way."

The mystery of faith: We trust God, and "somehow he takes the awfulness out of" the tragedy. What seemed unbearable ahead of time will somehow become bearable if and when the time comes.

In the end, I'm helpless to shield myself or my loved ones from the unthinkable. Yet there is this: the determination to apply faith to every present experience, easy and hard, pleasant and painful, so that if the floods cover me, I will not be swept away (see Isaiah 43:2).

Diane Eble

God's Words of Life *on*
FAMILY

A man will leave his father and mother and be united to his wife, and the two will become one flesh.

Ephesians 5:31

Train a child in the way he should go, and when he is old he will not turn from it.

Proverbs 22:6

Do not forget the things your eyes have seen or let them slip from your heart as long as you live. Teach them to your children and to their children after them.

Deuteronomy 4:9

The promise is for you and your children and for all who are far off—for all whom the Lord our God will call.

Acts 2:39

Jesus said: "Let the little children come to me, and do not hinder them, for the kingdom of God belongs to such as these."

Mark 10:14

Sons are a heritage from the LORD, children a reward from him. Like arrows in the hands of a warrior are sons born in one's youth. Blessed is the man whose quiver is full of them.

Psalm 127:3–5

God's Words of Life *on*
FAMILY

A woman giving birth to a child has pain because her time has come; but when her baby is born she forgets the anguish because of her joy that a child is born into the world.

John 16:21

I prayed for this child, and the LORD has granted me what I asked of him. So now I give him to the LORD. For his whole life he will be given over to the LORD.

1 Samuel 1:27–28

All your sons will be taught by the LORD, and great will be your children's peace.

Isaiah 54:13

Honor your father and mother ... that it may go well with you and that you may enjoy long life on the earth.

Ephesians 6:2–3

Both the one who makes men holy and those who are made holy are of the same family. So Jesus is not ashamed to call them brothers.

Hebrews 2:11

Whatever you did for one of the least of these brothers of mine, you did for me.

Matthew 25:40

God's Words of Life on
FAMILY

How good and pleasant it is when brothers
live together in unity!

Psalm 133:1

Anyone who does not love his brother, whom
he has seen, cannot love God, whom he has
not seen. And he has given us this command:
Whoever loves God must also love his brother.

1 John 4:20–21

STRONG FAMILIES PRODUCE STRONG CHILDREN

As our culture turns further away from God, we need stronger Christian families. Some parents see how bad the youth culture is and they panic and overreact. Or else they go to the other extreme and deny reality.

Parents need to avoid both of these extremes and face the facts head-on. Talk with your kids. Spend more time with them and not less. Love them more, not less, because the culture is constantly chipping away at their self-esteem. Hug your kids; build them up with your praise.

Beyond that, do everything you can to ground your children in the faith. Too many parents don't realize how powerful it is to help kids really walk with God. Kids want to know if the Christian faith actually works, and one way they can be shown that is to observe it working in the lives of their parents. In the end Christianity is not simply taught; it's caught. And if you ain't got it, they won't catch it.

So live for God—not simply for yourself but for your children and your children's children. God didn't put us here to win a popularity contest. He entrusted us with the task of raising godly children. And he gives us the power to make good on that responsibility.

Dawson McAllister

God's Words of Life *on*
FINANCES

The LORD is my shepherd, I shall not be in want.

Psalm 23:1

Turn my heart toward your statutes and not toward selfish gain.

Psalm 119:36

Why spend money on what is not bread, and your labor on what does not satisfy? Listen, listen to me, and eat what is good, and your soul will delight in the richest of fare.

Isaiah 55:2

No one can serve two masters. Either he will hate the one and love the other, or he will be devoted to the one and despise the other. You cannot serve both God and Money.

Matthew 6:24

Whoever trusts in his riches will fall, but the righteous will thrive like a green leaf.

Proverbs 11:28

Godliness with contentment is great gain. For we brought nothing into the world, and we can take nothing out of it. But if we have food and clothing, we will be content with that. . . . For the love of money is a root of all kinds of evil.

1 Timothy 6:6–8,10

God's Words of Life on
FINANCES

I know what it is to be in need, and I know what it is to have plenty. I have learned the secret of being content in any and every situation, whether well fed or hungry, whether living in plenty or in want.

Philippians 4:12

Jesus sat down opposite the place where the offerings were put and watched the crowd putting their money into the temple treasury. Many rich people threw in large amounts. But a poor widow came and put in two very small copper coins, worth only a fraction of a penny. Calling his disciples to him, Jesus said, "I tell you the truth, this poor widow has put more into the treasury than all the others. They all gave out of their wealth; but she, out of her poverty, put in everything—all she had to live on."

Mark 12:41–44

"Bring the whole tithe into the storehouse, that there may be food in my house. Test me in this," says the LORD Almighty, "and see if I will not throw open the floodgates of heaven and pour out so much blessing that you will not have room enough for it."

Malachi 3:10

God's Words of Life *on*
FINANCES

Jesus said: "Watch out! Be on your guard against all kinds of greed; a man's life does not consist in the abundance of his possessions."

Luke 12:15

Let no debt remain outstanding, except the continuing debt to love one another, for he who loves his fellowman has fulfilled the law.

Romans 13:8

Do not worry, saying, "What shall we eat?" or "What shall we drink?" or "What shall we wear?" For the pagans run after all these things, and your heavenly Father knows that you need them. But seek first his kingdom and his righteousness, and all these things will be given to you as well.

Matthew 6:31–33

Do not let this Book of the Law depart from your mouth; meditate on it day and night, so that you may be careful to do everything written in it. Then you will be prosperous and successful.

Joshua 1:8

A good man leaves an inheritance for his children's children, but a sinner's wealth is stored up for the righteous.

Proverbs 13:22

God's Words of Life on
FINANCES

Remember the LORD your God, for it is he who gives you the ability to produce wealth, and so confirms his covenant, which he swore to your forefathers, as it is today.

Deuteronomy 8:18

My God will meet all your needs according to his glorious riches in Christ Jesus.

Philippians 4:19

God is able to make all grace abound to you, so that in all things at all times, having all that you need, you will abound in every good work.

2 Corinthians 9:8

Store up for yourselves treasures in heaven, where moth and rust do not destroy, and where thieves do not break in and steal. For where your treasure is, there your heart will be also.

Matthew 6:20–21

If they obey and serve him, they will spend the rest of their days in prosperity and their years in contentment.

Job 36:11

God's Words of Life on
FINANCES

He who gathers money little by little makes it grow.

Proverbs 13:11

Whoever loves money never has money enough; whoever loves wealth is never satisfied with his income.

Ecclesiastes 5:10

Be shepherds of God's flock that is under your care, serving as overseers—not because you must, but because you are willing, as God wants you to be; not greedy for money, but eager to serve.

1 Peter 5:2

Keep your lives free from the love of money and be content with what you have, because God has said, "Never will I leave you; never will I forsake you."

Hebrews 13:5

Remember the LORD your God, for it is he who gives you the ability to produce wealth.

Deuteronomy 8:17

GOD CARES ABOUT OUR FINANCES

Richard and I both made career moves—ones we felt God's leading to make—which cut our income in half. I left a full-time job in favor of part-time work so I could be home with our kids more, and Richard resigned his job to pursue a career in real estate. Short-term projections said we could get by on our reduced income for some time. But it's been months now, and our expenses still exceed our income.

In the past, I had rarely included God in our financial decisions. Except for the percentage we gave to the church, I had figured our money was ours and if we messed up, it was our problem. With the exception of our mortgage, we had almost no debts. But perhaps we have failed to act responsibly by not recognizing that all we have truly does come from God and that he cares about every aspect of our life, including the water bill.

If I've learned anything by being broke, it's that there are still rooms in my life marked "private." God didn't lead us down this road to punish us for failing to relinquish every area of our life to him. But somehow for me, handing over the money behind "Door # 1" feels like the first hopeful step we've taken toward real financial freedom.

God's Words of Life on
FORGIVENESS

Then Peter came to Jesus and asked, "Lord, how many times shall I forgive my brother when he sins against me? Up to seven times?" Jesus answered, "I tell you, not seven times, but seventy-seven times."

Matthew 18:21–22

In him we have redemption through his blood, the forgiveness of sins, in accordance with the riches of God's grace.

Ephesians 1:7

You forgave the iniquity of your people and covered all their sins.

Psalm 85:2

God was reconciling the world to himself in Christ, not counting men's sins against them. And he has committed to us the message of reconciliation.

2 Corinthians 5:19

As far as the east is from the west, so far has he removed our transgressions from us.

Psalm 103:12

If we confess our sins, he is faithful and just and will forgive us our sins and purify us from all unrighteousness.

1 John 1:9

FORGIVENESS

I will forgive their wickedness and will remember their sins no more.

Hebrews 8:12

Let the wicked forsake his way and the evil man his thoughts. Let him turn to the LORD, and he will have mercy on him, and to our God, for he will freely pardon.

Isaiah 55:7

Bear with each other and forgive whatever grievances you may have against one another. Forgive as the LORD forgave you.

Colossians 3:13

When you stand praying, if you hold anything against anyone, forgive him, so that your Father in heaven may forgive you your sins.

Mark 11:25

I will cleanse them from all the sin they have committed against me and will forgive all their sins of rebellion against me.

Jeremiah 33:8

"Come now, let us reason together," says the LORD. "Though your sins are like scarlet, they shall be as white as snow; though they are red as crimson, they shall be like wool."

Isaiah 1:18

God's Words of Life *on*
FORGIVENESS

When you were dead in your sins and in the uncircumcision of your sinful nature, God made you alive with Christ. He forgave us all our sins.

Colossians 2:13

I, even I, am he who blots out your transgressions, for my own sake, and remembers your sins no more.

Isaiah 43:25

Blessed is he whose transgressions are forgiven, whose sins are covered. Blessed is the man whose sin the LORD does not count against him and in whose spirit is no deceit.

Psalm 32:1–2

I tell you the truth, all the sins and blasphemies of men will be forgiven them.

Mark 3:28

Once you were alienated from God and were enemies in your minds because of your evil behavior. But now he has reconciled you by Christ's physical body through death to present you holy in his sight, without blemish and free from accusation.

Colossians 1:21–22

Blessed are they whose transgressions are forgiven, whose sins are covered.

Romans 4:7

If my people, who are called by my name, will humble themselves and pray and seek my face and turn from their wicked ways, then will I hear from heaven and will forgive their sin and will heal their land.

2 Chronicles 7:14

Forgive, and you will be forgiven.

Luke 6:37

If anyone has caused grief ... you ought to forgive and comfort him, so that he will not be overwhelmed by excessive sorrow. I urge you, therefore, to reaffirm your love for him.

2 Corinthians 2:5, 7–8

For if you forgive men when they sin against you, your heavenly Father will also forgive you.

Matthew 6:14

Forgive us our debts, as we also have forgiven our debtors.

Matthew 6:12

God's Words of Life on
FORGIVENESS

Praise be to the God and Father of our Lord Jesus Christ! In his great mercy he has given us new birth into a living hope through the resurrection of Jesus Christ from the dead, and into an inheritance that can never perish, spoil or fade—kept in heaven for you.

1 Peter 1:3–4

Finally, all of you, live in harmony with one another; be sympathetic, love... be compassionate and humble.

1 Peter 3:8

Be kind and compassionate to one another, forgiving each other, just as in Christ God forgave you.

Ephesians 4:32

Accept one another, then, just as Christ accepted you, in order to bring praise to God.

Romans 15:7

BE QUICK TO FORGIVE

When forgiveness is necessary, don't wait too long. We must begin to forgive, because without forgiving, we choke off our own joy; we kill our own soul. People carrying hate and resentment can invest themselves so deeply in that resentment that they gradually define themselves in terms of it.

The longer you wait, the more you risk becoming a person defined by your anger, rather than simply a person who has a grievance. The offense and the resultant anger begin to possess you, until your identity is practically demonized by resentment.

When forgiveness is truly necessary, forgive as quickly as you can, because forgiving has two good results: the first is your own release, and the second is the possibility of reconciliation between you and your mate.

Lewis Smedes

God's Words of Life on
FRIENDSHIP

A friend loves at all times, and a brother is
born for adversity.

Proverbs 17:17

I no longer call you servants, because a servant does not know his master's business.
Instead, I have called you friends, for everything that I learned from my Father I have
made known to you.

John 15:15

A despairing man should have the devotion
of his friends.

Job 6:14

A man of many companions may come to
ruin, but there is a friend who sticks closer
than a brother.

Proverbs 18:24

My intercessor is my friend as my eyes pour
out tears to God.

Job 16:20

Do not make friends with a hot-tempered
man, do not associate with one easily
angered, or you may learn his ways and get
yourself ensnared.

Proverbs 22:24–25

Wounds from a friend can be trusted, but an enemy multiplies kisses.

Proverbs 27:6

Greater love has no one than this, that he lay down his life for his friends. You are my friends if you do what I command.

John 15:13–14

Perfume and incense bring joy to the heart, and the pleasantness of one's friend springs from his earnest counsel.

Proverbs 27:9

Jonathan had David reaffirm his oath out of love for him, because he loved him as he loved himself.

1 Samuel 20:17

Two are better than one, because they have a good return for their work: If one falls down, his friend can help him up. But pity the man who falls and has no one to help him up!

Ecclesiastes 4:9–10

Do two walk together unless they have agreed to do so?

Amos 3:3

God's Words of Life *on*
FRIENDSHIP

Dear friend, I pray that you may enjoy good health and that all may go well with you.

3 John 1:2

His mouth is sweetness itself; he is altogether lovely. This is my lover, this my friend.

Song of Songs 5:16

Do not forsake your friend and the friend of your father.

Proverbs 27:10

He who covers over an offense promotes love, but whoever repeats the matter separates close friends.

Proverbs 17:9

But it is you, ... my companion, my close friend, with whom I once enjoyed sweet fellowship as we walked with the throng at the house of God.

Psalm 55:13–14

A COVENANT OF FRIENDSHIP

Marriage is a covenant relationship—not a contract. By covenant, I mean marriage is a permanent commitment. Viewing marriage this way gives us security and freedom. Under covenant, I have a lifetime to learn how to bond together as one with my husband. The "I do" I said on my wedding day was not the culmination of a relationship, but the beginning of a new commitment to work on my relationship with my husband for the rest of my life.

Covenant provides us with the challenge to grow in our marriage. If I'm committed for the long haul, I can either live in solitude, emotionally divorcing myself, or I can build friendship with my husband by working on communication and continuing to discover new things about him.

In a sense, then, covenant encourages me to know my husband—and my husband to know me. And it gives us a lifetime to grow together in deep friendship.

Susan Alexander Yates

God's Words of Life on
GOALS

The plans of the diligent lead to profit as surely as haste leads to poverty.

Proverbs 21:5

The noble man makes noble plans, and by noble deeds he stands.

Isaiah 32:8

The plans of the righteous are just.

Proverbs 12:5

The LORD Almighty has sworn, "Surely, as I have planned, so it will be, and as I have purposed, so it will stand."

Isaiah 14:24

I know that you can do all things; no plan of yours can be thwarted.

Job 42:2

Do not those who plot evil go astray? But those who plan what is good find love and faithfulness.

Proverbs 14:22

Do I make my plans in a worldly manner so that in the same breath I say, "Yes, yes" and "No, no"?

2 Corinthians 1:17

Plans fail for lack of counsel, but with many advisers they succeed.

Proverbs 15:22

Make plans by seeking advice.

Proverbs 20:18

The LORD foils the plans of the nations; he thwarts the purposes of the peoples. But the plans of the LORD stand firm forever, the purposes of his heart through all generations.

Psalm 33:10–11

Do not put your trust in princes, in mortal men, who cannot save. When their spirit departs, they return to the ground; on that very day their plans come to nothing.

Psalm 146:3–4

Commit to the LORD whatever you do, and your plans will succeed.

Proverbs 16:3

Many are the plans in a man's heart, but it is the LORD's purpose that prevails.

Proverbs 19:21

There is no wisdom, no insight, no plan that can succeed against the LORD.

Proverbs 21:30

God's Words of Life *on*
GOALS

Whatever your hand finds to do, do it with all your might, for in the grave, where you are going, there is neither working nor planning nor knowledge nor wisdom.

Ecclesiastes 9:10

May he give you the desire of your heart and make all your plans succeed.

Psalm 20:4

GOALS

THE SHARED PURPOSE OF GOALS

You can develop a stronger sense of shared purpose in marriage by setting goals for the year ahead. Look at these seven areas of marital expectations. Rank them in order of importance to you. Then discuss your different expectations and explore ways you could improve your marriage.

1. *Security*: the knowledge of permanence in the relationship and of financial and material well-being.
2. *Companionship*: having common areas of interest and activity that you enjoy together.
3. *Sex*: the initiation and enjoyment of a growing physical relationship.
4. *Understanding and tenderness*: experiencing regularly a touch, a kiss, a wink across the room that says, "I love you, I care, I'm thinking of you."
5. *Encouragement*: verbal support and appreciation.
6. *Intellectual closeness*: discussing and growing together in common areas.
7. *Mutual activity*: doing things together, such as sports, church work, hobbies. In six months review your goals together. Use that time to evaluate and reshape them, as needed.

David and Claudia Arp & The Marriage
Partnership Staff

God's Words of Life on
HOPE

Be strong and take heart, all you who hope in the LORD.

Psalm 31:24

Faith is being sure of what we hope for and certain of what we do not see.

Hebrews 11:1

The eyes of the LORD are on those who fear him, on those whose hope is in his unfailing love.

Psalm 33:18

This I call to mind and therefore I have hope: Because of the LORD's great love we are not consumed, for his compassions never fail.

Lamentations 3:21–22

May the God of hope fill you with all joy and peace as you trust in him, so that you may overflow with hope by the power of the Holy Spirit.

Romans 15:13

May your unfailing love rest upon us, O LORD, even as we put our hope in you.

Psalm 33:22

Hope deferred makes the heart sick, but a longing fulfilled is a tree of life.

Proverbs 13:12

Now, LORD, what do I look for? My hope is in you.

Psalm 39:7

Why are you downcast, O my soul? Why so disturbed within me? Put your hope in God, for I will yet praise him, my Savior and my God.

Psalm 43:5

You have been my hope, O Sovereign LORD, my confidence since my youth.

Psalm 71:5

Everything that was written in the past was written to teach us, so that through endurance and the encouragement of the Scriptures we might have hope.

Romans 15:4

As for me, I will always have hope; I will praise you more and more.

Psalm 71:14

May our Lord Jesus Christ himself and God our Father, who loved us and by his grace gave us eternal encouragement and good hope, encourage your hearts and strengthen you in every good deed and word.

2 Thessalonians 2:16–17

God's Words of Life on
HOPE

May those who fear you rejoice when they see me, for I have put my hope in your word.

Psalm 119:74

We also rejoice in our sufferings, because we know that suffering produces perseverance; perseverance, character; and character, hope. And hope does not disappoint us, because God has poured out his love into our hearts by the Holy Spirit, whom he has given us.

Romans 5:3–5

Sustain me according to your promise, and I will live; do not let my hopes be dashed.

Psalm 119:116

Put your hope in the LORD, for with the LORD is unfailing love and with him is full redemption.

Psalm 130:7

Blessed is he whose help is the God of Jacob, whose hope is in the LORD his God, the Maker of heaven and earth, the sea, and everything in them—the LORD, who remains faithful forever.

Psalm 146:5–6

Know also that wisdom is sweet to your soul; if you find it, there is a future hope for you, and your hope will not be cut off.

Proverbs 24:14

God's Words of Life *on*
HOPE

Blessed is the man who trusts in the LORD, whose confidence is in him. He will be like a tree planted by the water that sends out its roots by the stream. It does not fear when heat comes; its leaves are always green. It has no worries in a year of drought and never fails to bear fruit.

Jeremiah 17:7–8

I say to myself, "The LORD is my portion; therefore I will wait for him." The LORD is good to those whose hope is in him, to the one who seeks him.

Lamentations 3:24–25

Hope that is seen is no hope at all. Who hopes for what he already has? But if we hope for what we do not yet have, we wait for it patiently.

Romans 8:24–25

Be joyful in hope.

Romans 12:12

We continually remember before our God and Father your work produced by faith, your labor prompted by love, and your endurance inspired by hope in our Lord Jesus Christ.

1 Thessalonians 1:3

God's Words of Life on
HOPE

We have this hope as an anchor for the soul, firm and secure. It enters the inner sanctuary behind the curtain.

Hebrews 6:19

In your hearts set apart Christ as Lord. Always be prepared to give an answer to everyone who asks you to give the reason for the hope that you have.

1 Peter 3:15

We say with confidence, "The LORD is my helper; I will not be afraid. What can man do to me?"

Hebrews 13:6

You will be secure, because there is hope; you will look about you and take your rest in safety.

Job 11:18

No one whose hope is in you will ever be put to shame.

Psalm 25:3

Guide me in your truth and teach me, for you are God my Savior, and my hope is in you all day long.

Psalm 25:5

We wait in hope for the LORD; he is our help and our shield.

Psalm 33:20

I will praise you forever for what you have done; in your name I will hope, for your name is good. I will praise you in the presence of your saints.

Psalm 52:9

Find rest, O my soul, in God alone; my hope comes from him.

Psalm 62:5

For you have been my hope, O Sovereign LORD, my confidence since my youth.

Psalm 71:5

You are my refuge and my shield; I have put my hope in your word.

Psalm 119:114

Even youths grow tired and weary, and young men stumble and fall; but those who hope in the LORD will renew their strength. They will soar on wings like eagles; they will run and not grow weary, they will walk and not be faint.

Isaiah 40:30–31

God's Words of Life on
HOPE

Then you will know that I am the LORD; those who hope in me will not be disappointed.

Isaiah 49:23

"For I know the plans I have for you," declares the LORD, "plans to prosper you and not to harm you, plans to give you hope and a future."

Jeremiah 29:11

By faith we eagerly await through the Spirit the righteousness for which we hope.

Galatians 5:5

Let us hold unswervingly to the hope we profess, for he who promised is faithful.

Hebrews 10:23

There is surely a future hope for you, and your hope will not be cut off.

Proverbs 23:18

I pray ... that the eyes of your heart may be enlightened in order that you may know the hope to which he has called you, the riches of his glorious inheritance in the saints, and his incomparably great power for us who believe.

Ephesians 1:18–19

CONQUERING DISAPPOINTMENT WITH HOPE

Disappointment can corrode a marriage like rust eats away at a car. Any number of things—a spouse's unemployment, a chronic illness, the loss of a child—these things often kill marriages.

This is where a spiritual perspective may not only help—but be essential. Faith does not deny disappointment. Some things really are awful. But look for answers we must. Renowned for his work with leprosy patients, Dr. Paul Brand responded to the question, "Where is God when it hurts?" with this: "He is in you, the one hurting, not in it, the thing that hurts."

We may find ourselves placing our hope in many things: our spouse, our children, our careers, our health. Yet these things have their limitations.

But God doesn't. Ultimately, our hope is in him. It's important to remember he is in us when we hurt. It is, perhaps, even more important to remember he is also in our spouse. The couples I have observed who have come through disappointment have done so first by God's grace, and second by holding firmly to each other. They have affirmed that the "we" is stronger than the "it" of disappointment. And their marriages are better for it.

Elizabeth Cody Newenhuyse   89

God's Words of Life on
HOSPITALITY

Offer hospitality to one another without grumbling. Each one should use whatever gift he has received to serve others, faithfully administering God's grace in its various forms.

1 Peter 4:9–10

Do not forget to entertain strangers, for by so doing some people have entertained angels without knowing it.

Hebrews 13:2

We ought therefore to show hospitality to such men so that we may work together for the truth.

3 John 8

I tell you the truth, anyone who gives you a cup of water in my name because you belong to Christ will certainly not lose his reward.

Mark 9:41

Jesus said, "I tell you the truth, whatever you did not do for one of the least of these, you did not do for me."

Matthew 25:45

Let us not love with words or tongue but with actions and in truth.

1 John 3:18

In everything I did, I showed you that by this kind of hard work we must help the weak, remembering the words the Lord Jesus himself said: "It is more blessed to give than to receive."

Acts 20:35

Share with God's people who are in need. Practice hospitality.

Romans 12:13

Is not this the kind of fasting I have chosen: to loose the chains of injustice and untie the cords of the yoke, to set the oppressed free and break every yoke? Is it not to share your food with the hungry and to provide the poor wanderer with shelter—when you see the naked, to clothe him, and not to turn away from your own flesh and blood? Then your light will break forth like the dawn, and your healing will quickly appear; then your righteousness will go before you, and the glory of the LORD will be your rear guard.

Isaiah 58:6–8

When an alien lives with you in your land, do not mistreat him. The alien living with you must be treated as one of your native-born. Love him as yourself, for you were aliens in Egypt. I am the LORD your God.

Leviticus 19:33–34

God's Words of Life on
HOSPITALITY

"I was hungry and you gave me something to eat, I was thirsty and you gave me something to drink, I was a stranger and you invited me in, I needed clothes and you clothed me, I was sick and you looked after me, I was in prison and you came to visit me." Then the righteous will answer him, "Lord, when did we see you hungry and feed you, or thirsty and give you something to drink? When did we see you a stranger and invite you in, or needing clothes and clothe you? When did we see you sick or in prison and go to visit you?" The King will reply, "I tell you the truth, whatever you did for one of the least of these brothers of mine, you did for me."

Matthew 25:35–40

Jesus said to his host, "When you give a luncheon or dinner, do not invite your friends, your brothers or relatives, or your rich neighbors; if you do, they may invite you back and so you will be repaid. But when you give a banquet, invite the poor, the crippled, the lame, the blind, and you will be blessed. Although they cannot repay you, you will be repaid at the resurrection of the righteous."

Luke 14:12–14

Be hospitable, one who loves what is good,
who is self-controlled, upright, holy and
disciplined.

Titus 1:8

Abraham looked up and saw three men
standing nearby. When he saw them, he hur-
ried from the entrance of his tent to meet
them and bowed low to the ground. He said,
"If I have found favor in your eyes, my lord,
do not pass your servant by. Let a little water
be brought, and then you may all wash your
feet and rest under this tree. Let me get you
something to eat, so you can be refreshed and
then go on your way—now that you have
come to your servant." "Very well," they
answered, "do as you say."

Genesis 18:2–5

If anyone serves, he should do it with the
strength God provides, so that in all things
God may be praised through Jesus Christ. To
him be the glory and the power for ever and
ever. Amen.

1 Peter 4:11

Do not forget to do good and to share with
others, for with such sacrifices God is
pleased.

Hebrews 13:16

God's Words of Life on
HOSPITALITY

But just as you excel in everything—in faith, in speech, in knowledge, in complete earnestness and in your love for us—see that you also excel in this grace of giving.

2 Corinthians 8:7

Do not withhold good from those who deserve it, when it is in your power to act.
Do not say to your neighbor,
"Come back later; I'll give it tomorrow"—
when you now have it with you.

Proverbs 3:27–28

A generous man will prosper; he who refreshes others will himself be refreshed.

Proverbs 11:25

Whoever is kind to the needy honors God.

Proverbs 14:31

SHARED HOSPITALITY

Tom, Martha and their children were leaving the next morning for an extended vacation, so we helped them empty their pantry. But a short while later unexpected guests arrived.

I followed Martha into the empty kitchen. She opened the refrigerator and took out a forgotten lettuce leaf. Then she unwrapped a three-day-old loaf of French bread, saying "A few drops of water and five minutes in the oven and it will be as good as new."

A corner of the refrigerator yielded up two hard-boiled eggs, which she peeled and chopped. There was a near-empty bottle of salad dressing. Martha dribbled a few drops of water into the bottle and smacked it until a dollop fell onto the eggs. We seasoned the "egg salad," spread it on the sliced bread, and slid the sandwiches under the broiler.

Martha set the table. The sandwiches and six leftover cookies sat next to a silver teapot. "The food is ready," Martha announced.

I looked at glowing faces and listened to lively reminiscences of the past and talk of future hopes. I thought of Jesus and his disciples and their simple suppers of bread and fish. On that chilly afternoon, I saw that the spirit of sharing is the essence of true hospitality. Even if you serve egg salad on old bread.

Donna Lobs

God's Words of Life *on*
ILLNESS

Praise the LORD, O my soul, and forget not all his benefits—who forgives all your sins and heals all your diseases, who redeems your life from the pit and crowns you with love and compassion.

Psalm 103:2–4

He took up our infirmities and carried our sorrows, yet we considered him stricken by God, smitten by him, and afflicted. But he was pierced for our transgressions, he was crushed for our iniquities; the punishment that brought us peace was upon him, and by his wounds we are healed.

Isaiah 53:4–5

Jesus went throughout Galilee, teaching in their synagogues, preaching the good news of the kingdom, and healing every disease and sickness among the people.

Matthew 4:23

The people all tried to touch him, because power was coming from him and healing them all.

Luke 6:19

Worship the LORD your God, and his blessing will be on your food and water. I will take away sickness from among you.

Exodus 23:25

A man with leprosy came and knelt before him and said, "Lord, if you are willing, you can make me clean." Jesus reached out his hand and touched the man. "I am willing," he said. "Be clean!" Immediately he was cured of his leprosy.

Matthew 8:2–3

Is any one of you sick? He should call the elders of the church to pray over him and anoint him with oil in the name of the Lord. And the prayer offered in faith will make the sick person well; the Lord will raise him up.

James 5:14–15

I pray that you may enjoy good health and that all may go well with you, even as your soul is getting along well.

3 John 2

Jesus went through all the towns and villages, teaching in their synagogues, preaching the good news of the kingdom and healing every disease and sickness.

Matthew 9:35

Heal me, O LORD, and I will be healed; save me and I will be saved, for you are the one I praise.

Jeremiah 17:14

God's Words of Life on
ILLNESS

If you listen carefully to the voice of the LORD your God and do what is right in his eyes, if you pay attention to his commands and keep all his decrees, I will not bring on you any of the diseases I brought on the Egyptians, for I am the LORD, who heals you.

Exodus 15:26

Heal the sick, raise the dead, cleanse those who have leprosy, drive out demons. Freely you have received, freely give.

Matthew 10:8

"I will restore you to health and heal your wounds," declares the LORD.

Jeremiah 30:17

Pay attention to what I say; listen closely to my words. Do not let them out of your sight, keep them within your heart; for they are life to those who find them and health to a man's whole body.

Proverbs 4:20–22

The centurion replied, "Lord, I do not deserve to have you come under my roof. But just say the word, and my servant will be healed."

Matthew 8:8

He sent forth his word and healed them; he rescued them from the grave.

Psalm 107:20

These signs will accompany those who believe: In my name they will drive out demons; they will speak in new tongues; they will pick up snakes with their hands; and when they drink deadly poison, it will not hurt them at all; they will place their hands on sick people, and they will get well.

Mark 16:17–18

A cheerful heart is good medicine, but a crushed spirit dries up the bones.

Proverbs 17:22

I will never forget your precepts, for by them you have preserved my life.

Psalm 119:93

You restored me to health and let me live.

Isaiah 38:16

Be merciful to me, LORD, for I am faint; O LORD, heal me, for my bones are in agony.

Psalm 6:2

For you who revere my name, the sun of righteousness will rise with healing in its wings.

Malachi 4:2

God's Words of Life *on*
ILLNESS

Pleasant words are a honeycomb, sweet to the soul and healing to the bones.

Proverbs 16:24

If my people, who are called by my name, will humble themselves and pray and seek my face and turn from their wicked ways, then will I hear from heaven and will forgive their sin and will heal their land.

2 Chronicles 7:14

They will turn to the LORD, and he will respond to their pleas and heal them.

Isaiah 19:22

"I will heal my people and will let them enjoy abundant peace and security."

Jeremiah 33:6

He heals the brokenhearted and binds up their wounds.

Psalm 147:3

IN SICKNESS AND IN HEALTH

When doctors discovered I had Lou Gehrig's Disease (ALS) in 1978, they gave me only a year to live. In the years since then, ALS has destroyed my voluntary muscle control.

One day when friends were waiting for me in the living room and my wife, Lucy, was helping me get ready, I suffered a bad coughing spell. I couldn't catch my breath, and I realized again what a terrible burden I was on my family. Tears of humiliation welled up, and I expressed to Lucy what I'd felt for a long time: "You and the children would be better off if I died."

But Lucy responded, "We would rather have you like this than not have you at all." I didn't know then how many times the memory of Lucy's words would give me the will to fight for my next breath.

Many loving husbands honestly say, "I couldn't live without my wife," but for me every single day I live is a testimony to God's grace and Lucy's devotion. If there's one thing Lucy and I have learned, it's this: Tomorrow is not promised to anyone. We're all terminal. Every day is a gift. And it's up to us to make the most of it.

Charlie Wedemeyer

God's Words of Life *on*
JOY

He will yet fill your mouth with laughter and
your lips with shouts of joy.

Job 8:21

His favor lasts a lifetime; weeping may
remain for a night, but rejoicing comes in the
morning.

Psalm 30:5

Rejoice in the LORD and be glad, you righteous; sing, all you who are upright in heart!

Psalm 32:11

Rejoice in the LORD your God, for he has
given you the autumn rains in righteousness.
He sends you abundant showers, both
autumn and spring rains.

Joel 2:23

Let the righteous rejoice in the LORD and take
refuge in him; let all the upright in heart
praise him!

Psalm 64:10

May all who seek you rejoice and be glad in
you; may those who love your salvation
always say, "Let God be exalted!"

Psalm 70:4

Though the fig tree does not bud and there are no grapes on the vines, though the olive crop fails and the fields produce no food, though there are no sheep in the pen and no cattle in the stalls, yet I will rejoice in the LORD, I will be joyful in God my Savior.

Habakkuk 3:17–18

Light is shed upon the righteous and joy on the upright in heart.

Psalm 97:11

The ransomed of the LORD will return. They will enter Zion with singing; everlasting joy will crown their heads. Gladness and joy will overtake them, and sorrow and sighing will flee away.

Isaiah 51:11

May the righteous be glad and rejoice before God; may they be happy and joyful.

Psalm 68:3

Let all who take refuge in you be glad; let them ever sing for joy. Spread your protection over them, that those who love your name may rejoice in you.

Psalm 5:11

God's Words of Life on
JOY

Shout for joy to the LORD, all the earth.
Worship the LORD with gladness; come before
him with joyful songs.

Psalm 100:1–2

May the God of hope fill you with all joy and
peace as you trust in him, so that you may
overflow with hope by the power of the Holy
Spirit.

Romans 15:13

I rejoice in following your statutes as one
rejoices in great riches.

Psalm 119:14

Rejoice that your names are written in heaven.

Luke 10:20

You have made known to me the paths of life;
you will fill me with joy in your presence.

Acts 2:28

Ask and you will receive, and your joy will
be complete.

John 16:24

Your statutes are my heritage forever; they
are the joy of my heart.

Psalm 119:111

Those who sow in tears will reap with songs of joy. He who goes out weeping, carrying seed to sow, will return with songs of joy, carrying sheaves with him.

Psalm 126:5–6

The prospect of the righteous is joy, but the hopes of the wicked come to nothing.

Proverbs 10:28

You will go out in joy and be led forth in peace; the mountains and hills will burst into song before you, and all the trees of the field will clap their hands.

Isaiah 55:12

Consider it pure joy, my brothers, whenever you face trials of many kinds, because you know that the testing of your faith develops perseverance.

James 1:2–3

Be joyful in hope, patient in affliction, faithful in prayer.

Romans 12:12

The kingdom of God is not a matter of eating and drinking, but of righteousness, peace and joy in the Holy Spirit.

Romans 14:17

God's Words of Life on
JOY

Rejoice in the Lord always. I will say it again:
Rejoice!

Philippians 4:4

Be joyful always.

1 Thessalonians 5:16

The joy of the LORD is your strength.

Nehemiah 8:10

THE JOY OF EVERYDAY THINGS

One bleak November afternoon I stood in the kitchen peeling carrots for soup, listening to the rhythmic thump of logs being stacked in the garage where my husband was replenishing the woodpile. One of our daughters knelt at the coffee table, writing her own novel. Another hummed to herself as she carefully cut out paper dolls from a sale catalogue. Suddenly I saw us just as we were—mother, father, wife, husband, children—and was stunned to the core by a surge of joy.

Paul told the Thessalonians to "Be joyful always . . . give thanks in all circumstances" (1 Thessalonians 5:16,18). We often interpret that as a call to endure, with grace, exceptionally difficult experiences or to embrace emotional pain with faith in God's power to heal and redeem us. But the same grace that blesses our deepest griefs can work in ordinary times too, reminding us that every day is a glory-fringed gift.

Tom and I try hard to call to each other's attention the goodness right here under our noses. Any healing love we're able to bring to our world will always be love that was nurtured in relationships at home—nurtured in the exchange of commonplace acts of love and care for each other.

Hope Harley

God's Words of Life on
KINDNESS

The LORD was with him; he showed him kindness.

Genesis 39:21

May the LORD show kindness to you, as you have shown ... to me.

Ruth 1:8

Blessed is he who is kind to the needy.

Proverbs 14:21

This is what the LORD Almighty says: "Administer true justice; show mercy and compassion to one another. Do not oppress the widow or the fatherless, the alien or the poor. In your hearts do not think evil of each other."

Zechariah 7:9–10

I have loved you with an everlasting love; I have drawn you with loving-kindness.

Jeremiah 31:3

Give to the one who asks you, and do not turn away from the one who wants to borrow from you.

Matthew 5:42

May the LORD now show you kindness and faithfulness.

2 Samuel 2:5

God's Words of Life on
KINDNESS

The King will say to those on his right,
"Come, you who are blessed by my Father;
take your inheritance, the kingdom prepared
for you since the creation of the world. For I
was hungry and you gave me something to
eat, I was thirsty and you gave me something
to drink, I was a stranger and you invited me
in, I needed clothes and you clothed me, I
was sick and you looked after me, I was in
prison and you came to visit me."

Matthew 25:34–36

Love is patient, love is kind. It does not envy,
it does not boast, it is not proud.

1 Corinthians 13:4

Carry each other's burdens, and in this way
you will fulfill the law of Christ.

Galatians 6:2

As God's chosen people, holy and dearly
loved, clothe yourselves with compassion,
kindness, humility, gentleness and patience.

Colossians 3:12

If anyone has material possessions and sees
his brother in need but has no pity on him,
how can the love of God be in him? Dear
children, let us not love with words or
tongue but with actions and in truth.

1 John 3:17–18

God's Words of Life *on*
KINDNESS

Live in harmony with one another; be sympathetic, love as brothers, be compassionate and humble. Do not repay evil with evil or insult with insult, but with blessing, because to this you were called so that you may inherit a blessing.

1 Peter 3:8–9

As we have opportunity, let us do good to all people, especially to those who belong to the family of believers.

Galatians 6:10

Make every effort to add to your faith goodness; and to goodness, knowledge; and to knowledge, self-control; and to self-control, perseverance; and to perseverance, godliness; and to godliness, brotherly kindness; and to brotherly kindness, love. For if you possess these qualities in increasing measure, they will keep you from being ineffective and unproductive in your knowledge of our Lord Jesus Christ.

2 Peter 1:5–8

Be kind and compassionate to one another, forgiving each other, just as in Christ God forgave you.

Ephesians 4:32

In everything, do to others what you would have them do to you, for this sums up the Law and the Prophets.

Matthew 7:12

May the LORD repay you for what you have done. May you be richly rewarded by the LORD.

Ruth 2:12

The fruit of the Spirit is love, joy, peace, patience, kindness, goodness, faithfulness.

Galatians 5:22

Love your enemies, do good to them, and lend to them without expecting to get anything back. Then your reward will be great, and you will be sons of the Most High, because he is kind to the ungrateful and wicked.

Luke 6:35

When the kindness and love of God our Savior appeared, he saved us, not because of righteous things we had done, but because of his mercy.

Titus 3:4–5

Love each other deeply, because love covers over a multitude of sins.

1 Peter 4:8

God's Words of Life on
KINDNESS

If anyone gives even a cup of cold water to one of these little ones because he is my disciple, I tell you the truth, he will certainly not lose his reward.

Matthew 10:42

I led them with cords of human kindness, with ties of love.

Hosea 11:4

No one has ever seen God; but if we love one another, God lives in us and his love is made complete in us.

1 John 4:12

Clothe yourselves with humility toward one another.

1 Peter 5:5

A KINDER, GENTLER LIFE

The Apostle Paul urged us to be kind and gentle toward one another (see Galatians 5:22–23). Sadly, I don't see either of these qualities in marriages much today. I don't see enough in my own marriage.

Is it kind to say, in front of your Bible study group, "Sorry we're late, but you know these women, especially after they hit 40!"? Is it gentle to assume that your wife naturally enjoys things like ironing, cooking, vacuuming and getting up in the middle of the night to care for a sick child? Is it kind and gentle to say, "You'll never find the time, and besides, we can't afford it," when your spouse says they are thinking about going back to school?

Many spouses will tell you the cold slap of a harsh answer hurts almost as bad as the back of the hand. Maybe more.

In Galatians, Paul uses fruit as a metaphor to describe what happens when Christ's Spirit resides in our hearts. It is a funny thing, this Spirit. Give him freedom to dwell within you, and there's little room for the grouchy words and thoughtless acts that bedevil many marriages.

Lyn Cryderman

Do not seek revenge or bear a grudge against one of your people, but love your neighbor as yourself. I am the LORD.

Leviticus 19:18

Love each other as I have loved you. Greater love has no one than this, that he lay down his life for his friends.

John 15:12–13

Be devoted to one another in brotherly love. Honor one another above yourselves.

Romans 12:10

In your unfailing love you will lead the people you have redeemed.

Exodus 15:13

Love each other.

John 15:17

Many waters cannot quench love; rivers cannot wash it away.

Song of Songs 8:7

Live a life of love, just as Christ loved us and gave himself up for us as a fragrant offering and sacrifice to God.

Ephesians 5:2

May the Lord make your love increase and overflow for each other and for everyone else, just as ours does for you.

1 Thessalonians 3:12

Keep on loving each other as brothers.

Hebrews 13:1

If you really keep the royal law found in Scripture, "Love your neighbor as yourself," you are doing right.

James 2:8

Place me like a seal over your heart, like a seal on your arm; for love is as strong as death,

Song of Songs 8:6

A new command I give you: Love one another. As I have loved you, so you must love one another. By this all men will know that you are my disciples.

John 13:34–35

Now that you have purified yourselves by obeying the truth so that you have sincere love for your brothers, love one another deeply, from the heart.

1 Peter 1:22

God's Words of Life *on*
LOVE

Live in harmony with one another; be sympathetic... be compassionate and humble.

1 Peter 3:9

For God did not give us a spirit of timidity, but a spirit of power, of love and of self-discipline.

2 Timothy 1:7

How beautiful you are and how pleasing, O love, with your delights!

Song of Songs 7:6

If I speak in the tongues of men and of angels, but have not love, I am only a resounding gong or a clanging cymbal. If I have the gift of prophecy and can fathom all mysteries and all knowledge, and if I have a faith that can move mountains, but have not love, I am nothing. If I give all I possess to the poor and surrender my body to the flames, but have not love, I gain nothing. Love is patient, love is kind. It does not envy, it does not boast, it is not proud. It is not rude, it is not self-seeking, it is not easily angered, it keeps no record of wrongs. Love does not delight in evil but rejoices with the truth. It always protects, always trusts, always hopes, always perseveres. Love never fails.

1 Corinthians 13:1–8

You yourselves have been taught by God to love each other.

1 Thessalonians 4:9

He has given us this command: Whoever loves God must also love his brother.

1 John 4:21

How delightful is your love ... my bride!

Song of Songs 4:10

Let us love one another, for love comes from God. Everyone who loves has been born of God and knows God. Whoever does not love does not know God, because God is love.

1 John 4:7–8

The fruit of the Spirit is love, joy, peace, patience, kindness, goodness, faithfulness.

Galatians 5:22

For God so loved the world that he gave his one and only Son, that whoever believes in him shall not perish but have eternal life.

John 3:16

He has taken me to the banquet hall, and his banner over me is love.

Song of Songs 2:4

God's Words of Life on
LOVE

Above all, love each other deeply, because love covers over a multitude of sins.

1 Peter 4:8

Keep yourselves in God's love as you wait for the mercy of our Lord Jesus Christ to bring you to eternal life.

Jude 1:21

No one has ever seen God; but if we love one another, God lives in us and his love is made complete in us.

1 John 4:12

And this is love: that we walk in obedience to his commands. As you have heard from the beginning, his command is that you walk in love.

2 John 1:6

Love covers over all wrongs.

Proverbs 10:12

Though the mountains be shaken, and the hills be removed, yet my unfailing love for you will not be shaken nor my covenant of peace be removed.

Isaiah 54:10

Neither height nor depth, nor anything else in all creation, will be able to separate us from the love of God that is in Christ Jesus our Lord.

Romans 8:39

Let him kiss me with the kisses of his mouth—for your love is more delightful than wine.

Song of Songs 1:2

Mercy, peace and love be yours in abundance.

Jude 1:2

All the ways of the LORD are loving and faithful for those who keep the demands of his covenant.

Psalm 25:10

He is my loving God and my fortress, my stronghold and my deliverer, my shield, in whom I take refuge.

Psalm 144:2

The LORD is faithful to all his promises and loving toward all he has made.

Psalm 145:13

God's Words of Life on
LOVE

May you rejoice in the wife of your youth . . .
may you ever be captivated by her love.

Proverbs 5:18–19

The LORD appeared to us . . . saying: "I have
loved you with an everlasting love; I have
drawn you with loving-kindness."

Jeremiah 31:3

All night long on my bed I looked for the one
my heart loves; I looked for him but did not
find him. I will get up now and go about the
city, through its streets and squares; I will
search for the one my heart loves. So I looked
for him but did not find him. The watchmen
found me as they made their rounds in the
city. "Have you seen the one my heart
loves?" Scarcely had I passed them when I
found the one my heart loves. I held him and
would not let him go.

Song of Songs 3:1–4

THE LANGUAGES OF LOVE

Each of us prefers certain "languages" to express and to accept appreciation and affection. My wife, Lynne, and I know this from experience.

For years we expressed love differently and didn't realize it. Because I appreciate people opening doors of opportunity for me, I assumed Lynne would too. I did everything I could to offer opportunities that would stimulate and inspire her. Finally she said, "Bill, I feel like you're never satisfied with what I'm doing. I wish that once in a while you would just put your arms around me, hold me and let me feel loved and accepted just the way I am."

Most of us mistakenly assume our spouses want to receive love the same way we do. So we use whatever language comes most naturally to us. And that usually doesn't work. I thought I was doing Lynne a favor, but in reality I was making her feel pressured and inadequate. What she actually needed was a loving embrace.

We must tell one another which love language communicates most clearly to us. Learning new ways of communicating love can transform a marriage where spouses hope they're loved into a marriage where they know they are.

Bill Hybels

God's Words of Life on
MID-LIFE CRISIS

Your strength will equal your days.

Deuteronomy 33:25

The LORD gives strength to his people; the LORD blesses his people with peace.

Psalm 29:11

I can do everything through him who gives me strength.

Philippians 4:13

Being strengthened with all power according to his glorious might so that you may have great endurance and patience.

Colossians 1:11

He has made everything beautiful in its time. He has also set eternity in the hearts of men.

Ecclesiastes 3:11

I pray that out of his glorious riches he may strengthen you with power through his Spirit in your inner being, so that Christ may dwell in your hearts through faith. And I pray that you, being rooted and established in love, may have power, together with all the saints, to grasp how wide and long and high and deep is the love of Christ.

Ephesians 3:16–18

"Not by might nor by power, but by my Spirit," says the LORD Almighty.

Zechariah 4:6

In your unfailing love you will lead the people you have redeemed. In your strength you will guide them.

Exodus 15:13

Let the morning bring me word of your unfailing love, for I have put my trust in you. Show me the way I should go, for to you I lift up my soul.

Psalm 143:8

Test me, O LORD, and try me, examine my heart and my mind; for your love is ever before me, and I walk continually in your truth.

Psalm 26:2–3

Since you are my rock and my fortress, for the sake of your name lead and guide me.

Psalm 31:3

Teach me your ways so I may know you and continue to find favor with you.

Exodus 33:13

God's Words of Life *on*
MID-LIFE CRISIS

Teach me your way, O LORD, and I will walk in your truth; give me an undivided heart, that I may fear your name.

Psalm 86:11

Teach me, O LORD, to follow your decrees; then I will keep them to the end. Give me understanding, and I will keep your law and obey it with all my heart. Direct me in the path of your commands, for there I find delight. Turn my heart toward your statutes and not toward selfish gain. Turn my eyes away from worthless things; preserve my life according to your word.

Psalm 119:33–37

May the Lord direct your hearts into God's love and Christ's perseverance.

2 Thessalonians 3:5

The LORD will guide you always; he will satisfy your needs in a sun-scorched land and will strengthen your frame. You will be like a well-watered garden, like a spring whose waters never fail.

Isaiah 58:11

He knows the way that I take; when he has tested me, I will come forth as gold.

Job 23:10

You know that the testing of your faith develops perseverance. Perseverance must finish its work so that you may be mature and complete, not lacking anything.

James 1:3–4

Praise the LORD, O my soul, and forget not all his benefits—who forgives all your sins and heals all your diseases, who redeems your life from the pit and crowns you with love and compassion, who satisfies your desires with good things so that your youth is renewed like the eagle's.

Psalm 103:2–5

Peace I leave with you; my peace I give you.

John 14:27

Do not be anxious about anything, but in everything, by prayer and petition, with thanksgiving, present your requests to God. And the peace of God, which transcends all understanding, will guard your hearts and your minds in Christ Jesus.

Philippians 4:6–7

Do not let your hearts be troubled. Trust in God.

John 14:1

God's Words of Life on
MID-LIFE CRISIS

Be strong and take heart, all you who hope in the LORD.

Psalm 31:24

Praise be to the God and Father of our Lord Jesus Christ, the Father of compassion and the God of all comfort, who comforts us in all our troubles, so that we can comfort those in any trouble with the comfort we ourselves have received from God.

2 Corinthians 1:3–4

Set your minds on things above, not on earthly things.

Colossians 3:2

"For my thoughts are not your thoughts, neither are your ways my ways," declares the LORD. "As the heavens are higher than the earth, so are my ways higher than your ways and my thoughts than your thoughts."

Isaiah 55:8–9

Praise and exalt and glorify the King of heaven, because everything he does is right and all his ways are just.

Daniel 4:37

The fear of the LORD adds length to life, but the years of the wicked are cut short.

Proverbs 10:27

TOGETHERNESS TIME

The couples who have long-term, happy marriages are the ones who make sure they have "togetherness time" on a regular basis. If careers and parenting responsibilities crowd their evening hours, they need to make time for each other in the mornings. Schedule a breakfast appointment at a restaurant, for example, where you can get caught up with each other's lives.

If your marriage has become stale, there's no better time than now to start doing romantic things and establishing stronger emotional connectedness that will make your relationship more satisfying. It's important that you do this, because over a period of years you're going to go through several crises together. Things will happen with your children that will either be disappointments or tragedies. Your parents are aging, and it's likely that at least one of them will die sooner than you expected them to. And there's always the mid-life re-evaluation, which can be traumatic.

It's important that you have your marriage relationship working well so you can make it through these tough times.

Jim and Sally Conway

God's Words of Life *on*
OBEDIENCE

This is how we know that we love the children of God: by loving God and carrying out his commands. This is love for God: to obey his commands. And his commands are not burdensome.

1 John 5:2–3

We will serve the LORD our God and obey him.

Joshua 24:24

If you walk in my ways and obey my statutes and commands ... I will give you a long life.

1 Kings 3:14

This is love: that we walk in obedience to his commands. As you have heard from the beginning, his command is that you walk in love.

2 John 6

I have considered my ways and have turned my steps to your statutes. I will hasten and not delay to obey your commands.

Psalm 119:59–60

Those who obey his commands live in him, and he in them. And this is how we know that he lives in us: We know it by the Spirit he gave us.

1 John 3:24

All the ways of the LORD are loving and faithful for those who keep the demands of his covenant.

Psalm 25:10

I have kept my feet from every evil path so that I might obey your word.

Psalm 119:101

From everlasting to everlasting the LORD's love is with those who fear him, and his righteousness with their children's children—with those who keep his covenant and remember to obey his precepts.

Psalm 103:17–18

We know that we have come to know him if we obey his commands. The man who says, "I know him," but does not do what he commands is a liar, and the truth is not in him. But if anyone obeys his word, God's love is truly made complete in him.

1 John 2:3–5

Therefore, my dear friends, as you have always obeyed—not only in my presence, but now much more in my absence—continue to work out your salvation with fear and trembling, for it is God who works in you to will and to act according to his good purpose.

Philippians 2:12–13

God's Words of Life on
OBEDIENCE

Blessed are they who keep his statutes and seek him with all their heart. They do nothing wrong; they walk in his ways.

Psalm 119:2–3

To obey is better than sacrifice, and to heed is better than the fat of rams.

1 Samuel 15:22

He who obeys instructions guards his life.

Proverbs 19:16

If our hearts do not condemn us, we have confidence before God and receive from him anything we ask, because we obey his commands and do what pleases him.

1 John 3:21–22

Whoever has my commands and obeys them, he is the one who loves me. He who loves me will be loved by my Father, and I too will love him and show myself to him.

John 14:21

If you love me, you will obey what I command.

John 14:15

Blessed . . . are those who hear the word of God and obey it.

Luke 11:28

Obey me, and I will be your God and you will be my people. Walk in all the ways I command you, that it may go well with you.

Jeremiah 7:23

Anyone who breaks one of the least of these commandments and teaches others to do the same will be called least in the kingdom of heaven, but whoever practices and teaches these commands will be called great in the kingdom of heaven.

Matthew 5:19

Jesus said: "If anyone loves me, he will obey my teaching. My Father will love him, and we will come to him and make our home with him. He who does not love me will not obey my teaching."

John 14:23–24

If you obey my commands, you will remain in my love, just as I have obeyed my Father's commands and remain in his love.

John 15:10

Obey your leaders and submit to their authority. They keep watch over you as men who must give an account. Obey them so that their work will be a joy, not a burden.

Hebrews 13:16–17

God's Words of Life *on*
OBEDIENCE

Do not merely listen to the word, and so deceive yourselves. Do what it says. Anyone who listens to the word but does not do what it says is like a man who looks at his face in a mirror and, after looking at himself, goes away and immediately forgets what he looks like.

James 1:22–24

Reform your ways and your actions and obey the LORD your God.

Jeremiah 26:13

Be very strong; be careful to obey all that is written in the Book of the Law of Moses, without turning aside to the right or to the left.

Joshua 23:6

You have declared this day that the LORD is your God and that you will walk in his ways, that you will keep his decrees, commands and laws, and that you will obey him.

Deuteronomy 26:17

Be careful that you do not forget the LORD your God, failing to observe his commands, his laws and his decrees that I am giving you this day. Otherwise, when you eat and are satisfied . . . and all you have is multiplied, then your heart will become proud and you will forget the LORD your God.

Deuteronomy 8:11–14

THE TOTAL SURRENDER OF OBEDIENCE

We were faced with a decision to move. I believed that if we followed the concrete, visible guidance in our daily lives, God would honor us. He would put us in the right place at the right time.

Catherine Marshall once noted that when a person finally comes to a place in her prayer life where she says, "'God, whatever you want for my life now, I accept it,' then God really begins to work. But first, one must give up self-will and be willing to totally accept God's will, no matter what it is."

Jesus prayed in the Garden of Gethsemane: "My Father, if it is possible, may this cup be taken from me. Yet not as I will, but as you will" (Matthew 26:39). From that total surrender came the most precious sacrifice ever made. Compared to such a surrender, what was I giving up?

Randy and I moved to Utah. Our new home was in a lush green valley, not the desert I had imagined. We were surrounded by loving, warm people, and even an airport close by so I could fly home occasionally. God cares for the little things in our lives—if only we'll surrender the big ones.

Alesia T. Thayer

God's Words of Life on
PATIENCE

Be still before the LORD and wait patiently for him; do not fret when men succeed in their ways, when they carry out their wicked schemes.

Psalm 37:7

A hot-tempered man stirs up dissension, but a patient man calms a quarrel.

Proverbs 15:18

The end of a matter is better than its beginning, and patience is better than pride. Do not be quickly provoked in your spirit, for anger resides in the lap of fools.

Ecclesiastes 7:8–9

It is good to wait quietly for the salvation of the LORD.

Lamentations 3:26

Wait for the LORD; be strong and take heart and wait for the LORD.

Psalm 27:14

You need to persevere so that when you have done the will of God, you will receive what he has promised.

Hebrews 10:36

Be joyful in hope, patient in affliction, faithful in prayer.

Romans 12:12

Since we are surrounded by such a great cloud of witnesses, let us throw off everything that hinders and the sin that so easily entangles, and let us run with perseverance the race marked out for us.

Hebrews 12:1

The testing of your faith develops perseverance. Perseverance must finish its work so that you may be mature and complete, not lacking anything.

James 1:3–4

If we hope for what we do not yet have, we wait for it patiently.

Romans 8:25

Be patient, then, brothers, until the Lord's coming. See how the farmer waits for the land to yield its valuable crop and how patient he is for the autumn and spring rains. You too, be patient and stand firm, because the Lord's coming is near.

James 5:7–8

God's Words of Life on
PATIENCE

Love is patient, love is kind. It does not envy, it does not boast, it is not proud.

1 Corinthians 13:4

Let us not become weary in doing good, for at the proper time we will reap a harvest if we do not give up.

Galatians 6:9

Be completely humble and gentle; be patient, bearing with one another in love.

Ephesians 4:2

As God's chosen people, holy and dearly loved, clothe yourselves with compassion, kindness, humility, gentleness and patience.

Colossians 3:12

I was shown mercy so that in me, the worst of sinners, Christ Jesus might display his unlimited patience as an example for those who would believe on him and receive eternal life.

1 Timothy 1:16

The Lord is not slow in keeping his promise, as some understand slowness. He is patient with you, not wanting anyone to perish, but everyone to come to repentance.

2 Peter 3:9

Everyone should be quick to listen, slow to speak and slow to become angry, for man's anger does not bring about the righteous life that God desires.

James 1:19–20

I wait for the LORD, my soul waits, and in his word I put my hope. My soul waits for the Lord more than watchmen wait for the morning, more than watchmen wait for the morning.

Psalm 130:5–6

Live a life worthy of the Lord ... please him in every way: bearing fruit in every good work, growing in the knowledge of God, being strengthened with all power according to his glorious might so that you may have great endurance and patience.

Colossians 1:10–11

Warn those who are idle, encourage the timid, help the weak, be patient with everyone.

1 Thessalonians 5:14

The fruit of the Spirit is love, joy, peace, patience, kindness, goodness, faithfulness, gentleness and self-control. Against such things there is no law.

Galatians 5:22–23

God's Words of Life *on*
PATIENCE

Make every effort to add to your faith goodness; and to goodness, knowledge; and to
knowledge, self-control; and to self-control,
perseverance; and to perseverance, godliness.

2 Peter 1:5–6

A man's wisdom gives him patience; it is to
his glory to overlook an offense.

Proverbs 19:11

Patience is better than pride.

Ecclesiastes 7:8

Preach the Word; be prepared in season and
out of season; correct, rebuke and encourage—
with great patience and careful instruction.

2 Timothy 4:2

Imitate those who through faith and patience
inherit what has been promised.

Hebrews 6:12

Bear in mind that our Lord's patience means
salvation.

2 Peter 3:15

Keep yourselves in God's love as you wait
for the mercy of our Lord Jesus Christ to
bring you to eternal life.

Jude 1:21

A Spouse's Patience

I've been married more than forty-five years, and I can testify to the truth that self-fulfillment is reached most surely and most richly by not seeking it. I went through a period in my forties and early fifties when, if it hadn't been for my wife's patience and loyalty and love, our marriage would have dissolved.

At that time our daughter was an adolescent hothead, a volcano of anger directed toward her birth-mother, who had given her up for adoption years earlier. Both Doris and I were deeply pained and frustrated, each not understanding how the other was handling the pain of our adopted daughter's anger. And I, at the same time, was prey to the feeling that I was being cheated out of some of the happiness I'd dreamed of having. I became a very, very angry person. But fortunately, Doris believed in God and in God's patience with angry fathers. Her patience with me and her faith in God made my own recovery possible, and it preserved our marriage. Today, I can't begin to tell you how grateful I am for her patience and long-suffering toward me.

Lewis Smedes

God's Words of Life on
PEACE

You will keep in perfect peace him whose mind is steadfast, because he trusts in you.

Isaiah 26:3

The LORD gives strength to his people; the LORD blesses his people with peace.

Psalm 29:11

He himself is our peace.

Ephesians 2:14

LORD, you establish peace for us; all that we have accomplished you have done for us.

Isaiah 26:12

Let the peace of Christ rule in your hearts, since as members of one body you were called to peace. And be thankful.

Colossians 3:15

I will lie down and sleep in peace, for you alone, O LORD, make me dwell in safety.

Psalm 4:8

Do not be anxious about anything, but in everything, by prayer and petition, with thanksgiving, present your requests to God. And the peace of God, which transcends all understanding, will guard your hearts and your minds in Christ Jesus.

Philippians 4:6–7

Turn from evil and do good; seek peace and pursue it.

Psalm 34:14

The fruit of the Spirit is love, joy, peace, patience, kindness, goodness, faithfulness.

Galatians 5:22

The meek will inherit the land and enjoy great peace.

Psalm 37:11

Great peace have they who love your law, and nothing can make them stumble.

Psalm 119:165

Aim for perfection, listen to my appeal, be of one mind, live in peace. And the God of love and peace will be with you.

2 Corinthians 13:11

Peace I leave with you; my peace I give you. I do not give to you as the world gives. Do not let your hearts be troubled and do not be afraid.

John 14:27

Make every effort to keep the unity of the Spirit through the bond of peace.

Ephesians 4:3

God's Words of Life on
PEACE

If it is possible, as far as it depends on you, live at peace with everyone.

Romans 12:18

The wisdom that comes from heaven is first of all pure; then peace-loving, considerate, submissive, full of mercy and good fruit, impartial and sincere. Peacemakers who sow in peace raise a harvest of righteousness.

James 3:17–18

Submit to God and be at peace with him; in this way prosperity will come to you.

Job 22:21

THE GRACE OF PEACE

Ken and I just had a quarrel. An hour pass-
es, and Ken enters the room. "I can't stand
it when you come on with that strong-willed
tone of yours," he says. "I know it's because
you're a survivor, a fighter. But I just can't
handle you like that."

"I feel like every time the slightest conflict
surfaces, you back off," I tell him.

"Maybe the only thing to do now is pray,"
Ken suggests. He mumbles a few phrases,
mechanically saying things about God's great-
ness, holiness and mercy. But I hear his heart
begin to soften as he finishes.

My prayer begins just as hollow-sounding
as his. But after several moments I too sense
my heart beginning to melt.

Ken takes a deep breath. "I can't believe
this," he says. "A load of concrete is off of me.
I feel so light."

"That's amazing," I tell him. "Just seconds
ago I felt the same peace and contentment."
Without thinking I utter the words, "I love
you." Ken embraces me, burying his head into
my shoulder. We feel a sense of wonder at how
strong Ken is when I am weak; at how weak
Ken is when I am strong; and how God, with his
strength, keeps us both from falling from grace.

Joni Eareckson Tada

God's Words of Life *on*
PRAYER

Again, I tell you that if two of you on earth agree about anything you ask for, it will be done for you by my Father in heaven. For where two or three come together in my name, there am I with them.

Matthew 18:19–20

Before they call I will answer; while they are still speaking I will hear.

Isaiah 65:24

Ask and it will be given to you; seek and you will find; knock and the door will be opened to you. For everyone who asks receives; he who seeks finds; and to him who knocks, the door will be opened.

Matthew 7:7–8

Dear friends, if our hearts do not condemn us, we have confidence before God and receive from him anything we ask, because we obey his commands and do what pleases him.

1 John 3:21–22

When you pray, go into your room, close the door and pray to your Father, who is unseen. Then your Father, who sees what is done in secret, will reward you.

Matthew 6:6

God's Words of Life on
PRAYER

The LORD is near to all who call on him, to all who call on him in truth.

Psalm 145:18

Call to me and I will answer you and tell you great and unsearchable things you do not know.

Jeremiah 33:3

He will call upon me, and I will answer him; I will be with him in trouble, I will deliver him and honor him.

Psalm 91:15

If you believe, you will receive whatever you ask for in prayer.

Matthew 21:22

The LORD is far from the wicked but he hears the prayer of the righteous.

Proverbs 15:29

Delight yourself in the LORD and he will give you the desires of your heart.

Psalm 37:4

Whatever you ask for in prayer, believe that you have received it, and it will be yours.

Mark 11:24

God's Words of Life *on*
PRAYER

Let us then approach the throne of grace with confidence, so that we may receive mercy and find grace to help us in our time of need.

Hebrews 4:16

I tell you the truth, my Father will give you whatever you ask in my name. Until now you have not asked for anything in my name. Ask and you will receive, and your joy will be complete.

John 16:23–24

If my people, who are called by my name, will humble themselves and pray and seek my face and turn from their wicked ways, then will I hear from heaven and will forgive their sin and will heal their land.

2 Chronicles 7:14

If we confess our sins, he is faithful and just and will forgive us our sins and purify us from all unrighteousness.

1 John 1:9

Very early in the morning, while it was still dark, Jesus got up, left the house and went off to a solitary place, where he prayed.

Mark 1:35

Jesus told his disciples a parable to show them that they should always pray and not give up.

Luke 18:1

If you remain in me and my words remain in you, ask whatever you wish, and it will be given you.

John 15:7

I will do whatever you ask in my name, so that the Son may bring glory to the Father. You may ask me for anything in my name, and I will do it.

John 14:13–14

Is any one of you in trouble? He should pray. Is anyone happy? Let him sing songs of praise. Is any one of you sick? He should call the elders of the church to pray over him and anoint him with oil in the name of the Lord. And the prayer offered in faith will make the sick person well; the Lord will raise him up. If he has sinned, he will be forgiven. Therefore confess your sins to each other and pray for each other so that you may be healed. The prayer of a righteous man is powerful and effective.

James 5:13–16

God's Words of Life on
PRAYER

This is the confidence we have in approaching God: that if we ask anything according to his will, he hears us. And if we know that he hears us—whatever we ask—we know that we have what we asked of him.

1 John 5:14–15

I wait for you, O LORD; you will answer, O Lord my God.

Psalm 38:15

The eyes of the Lord are on the righteous and his ears are attentive to their prayer.

1 Peter 3:12

THE STRENGTH OF PRAYER

An important aspect of a married person's prayer life has to be praying with your spouse. Prayer is the cement that holds a marriage together. The hurts and misunderstandings that come into all marriages melt away in the presence of a holy God.

When you stand before God, there is no room for pride or anger or resentful feelings. Rather, there is power in your marriage and in your lives as the two of you agree together in prayer.

Praying with my husband, Chris, is a humbling experience. We often kneel and hold hands. When we invite the Holy God into our marriage, into our home, into our bedroom where we pray, it is bound to draw us together.

Living a life of prayer is the power source of all Christians. It provides us with the resources to be the persons God would have us be.

Evelyn Christenson

God's Words of Life *on*
PRIORITIES

Let us throw off everything that hinders and the sin that so easily entangles, and let us run with perseverance the race marked out for us. Let us fix our eyes on Jesus, the author and perfecter of our faith, who for the joy set before him endured the cross, scorning its shame, and sat down at the right hand of the throne of God.

Hebrews 12:1–2

Seek first his kingdom and his righteousness, and all these things will be given to you as well.

Matthew 6:33

Jesus said: "This, then, is how you should pray: 'Our Father in heaven, hallowed be your name, your kingdom come, your will be done on earth as it is in heaven.'"

Matthew 6:9–10

By faith Moses, when he had grown up, refused to be known as the son of Pharaoh's daughter. He chose to be mistreated along with the people of God rather than to enjoy the pleasures of sin for a short time. He regarded disgrace for the sake of Christ as of greater value than the treasures of Egypt, because he was looking ahead to his reward.

Hebrews 11:24–26

I consider my life worth nothing to me, if only I may finish the race and complete the task the Lord Jesus has given me—the task of testifying to the gospel of God's grace.

Acts 20:24

Blessed is the man who does not walk in the counsel of the wicked or stand in the way of sinners or sit in the seat of mockers. But his delight is in the law of the LORD, and on his law he meditates day and night.

Psalm 1:1–2

Jesus said: "I tell you, use worldly wealth to gain friends for yourselves, so that when it is gone, you will be welcomed into eternal dwellings. Whoever can be trusted with very little can also be trusted with much, and whoever is dishonest with very little will also be dishonest with much. So if you have not been trustworthy in handling worldly wealth, who will trust you with true riches?"

Luke 16:9–11

Whatever was to my profit I now consider loss for the sake of Christ.

Philippians 3:7

The only thing that counts is faith expressing itself through love.

Galatians 5:6

God's Words of Life on
PRIORITIES

Someone will say, "You have faith; I have deeds." Show me your faith without deeds, and I will show you my faith by what I do.

James 2:18

Let us not love with words or tongue but with actions and in truth.

1 John 3:18

Make my joy complete by being like-minded, having the same love, being one in spirit and purpose. Do nothing out of selfish ambition or vain conceit, but in humility consider others better than yourselves. Each of you should look not only to your own interests, but also to the interests of others. Your attitude should be the same as that of Christ Jesus.

Philippians 2:2–5

We fix our eyes not on what is seen, but on what is unseen. For what is seen is temporary, but what is unseen is eternal.

2 Corinthians 4:18

Whatever you do, work at it with all your heart, as working for the Lord, not for men, since you know that you will receive an inheritance from the Lord as a reward. It is the Lord Christ you are serving.

Colossians 3:23–24

FIRST THINGS FIRST

When God's people returned from exile, they went about the task of building homes for their families. Sounds like a reasonable decision, doesn't it? Well, it didn't make sense to God.

The Lord wasn't pleased that his people focused so quickly on building their own homes. God told them, "I called forth a drought on the fields ... and on the labor of your hands" (Haggai 1:11). As long as God's house—the temple in Jerusalem—stood in ruins, the work of his people would never prosper.

It's often the good things in life—building a home, working with the PTA, pursuing a hobby—that distract our focus from the Kingdom of God. We're behind at work, the drain in the kitchen is leaking, and relatives are coming for the holidays. Certainly, there's a place for all of these things in our lives. But the key is knowing where that place is.

Once God's people set to work rebuilding the temple, the Lord honored their obedience in two ways. First, he encouraged them with his presence. Second, he blessed them (see Haggai 2:5,19).

When our marriages hit a dry period, it could be that we've lost sight of God's legitimate claim to be first in our lives.

Ron and Jeanette Lee

God's Words of Life on
ROMANCE

I found the one my heart loves. I held him and would not let him go.

Song of Songs 3:4

Enjoy life with your wife, whom you love, all the days ... that God has given you under the sun.

Ecclesiastes 9:9

Love each other deeply, because love covers over a multitude of sins.

1 Peter 4:8

If a man has recently married, he must not be sent to war or have any other duty laid on him. For one year he is to be free to stay at home and bring happiness to the wife he has married.

Deuteronomy 24:5

Husbands ought to love their wives as their own bodies. He who loves his wife loves himself.

Ephesians 5:28

How beautiful you are, my darling! Oh, how beautiful! Your eyes are doves. How handsome you are, my lover! Oh, how charming!

Song of Songs 1:15–16

The LORD God said, "It is not good for the man to be alone. I will make a helper suitable for him."

Genesis 2:18

He who finds a wife finds what is good and receives favor from the LORD.

Proverbs 18:22

Marriage should be honored by all.

Hebrews 13:4

Live a life of love, just as Christ loved us and gave himself up for us as a fragrant offering and sacrifice to God.

Ephesians 5:2

May you rejoice in the wife of your youth.

Proverbs 5:18

[Love] always protects, always trusts, always hopes, always perseveres. Love never fails.

1 Corinthians 13:7–8

Place me like a seal over your heart, like a seal on your arm; for love is as strong as death.

Song of Songs 8:6

I belong to my lover and his desire is for me.

Song of Songs 7:10

God's Words of Life on
ROMANCE

The man said, "This is now bone of my bones and flesh of my flesh; she shall be called 'woman,' for she was taken out of man." For this reason a man will leave his father and mother and be united to his wife, and they will become one flesh.

Genesis 2:23–24

Come, my lover, let us go to the countryside, let us spend the night in the villages. Let us go early to the vineyards to see if the vines have budded, if their blossoms have opened, and if the pomegranates are in bloom—there I will give you my love.

Song of Songs 7:11–12

Love one another, for love comes from God.

1 John 4:7

Each one of you also must love his wife as he loves himself, and the wife must respect her husband.

Ephesians 5:33

How beautiful you are and how pleasing, O love, with your delights!

Song of Songs 7:6

Since God so loved us, we also ought to love one another.

1 John 4:11

God's Words of Life *on*
ROMANCE

Jacob was in love with Rachel . . . So Jacob
served seven years to get Rachel, but they
seemed like only a few days to him because
of his love for her.

Genesis 29:18,20

How much more pleasing is your love than
wine, and the fragrance of your perfume than
any spice!

Song of Songs 4:10

Spur one another on toward love and good
deeds.

Hebrews 10:24

I will betroth you to me forever; I will betroth
you in righteousness and justice, in love and
compassion. I will betroth you in faithfulness,
and you will acknowledge the LORD.

Hosea 2:19–20

My lover spoke and said to me, "Arise, my
darling, my beautiful one, and come with me.
See! The winter is past; the rains are over and
gone. Flowers appear on the earth; the season
of singing has come, the cooing of doves is
heard in our land. The fig tree forms its early
fruit; the blossoming vines spread their fragrance. Arise, come, my darling; my beautiful
one, come with me."

Song of Songs 2:10–13

God's Words of Life on
ROMANCE

There are three things that are too amazing for me, four that I do not understand: the way of an eagle in the sky, the way of a snake on a rock, the way of a ship on the high seas, and the way of a man with a maiden.

Proverbs 30:18–19

Let him kiss me with the kisses of his mouth— for your love is more delightful than wine.

Song of Songs 1:2

Pleasing is the fragrance of your perfumes; your name is like perfume poured out.

Song of Songs 1:3

Like a lily among thorns is my darling among the maidens.

Song of Songs 2:2

Strengthen me with raisins, refresh me with apples, for I am faint with love.

Song of Songs 2:5

His left arm is under my head, and his right arm embraces me.

Song of Songs 2:6

All beautiful you are, my darling; there is no flaw in you.

Song of Songs 4:7

THE ELEMENTS OF ROMANCE

Romance can be constantly present in marriage, although its intensity will vary. There are peak moments, such as in physical lovemaking. But there are major portions of time when romance is no more intense than a smile or a gentle touch.

Daily romance is built upon qualities that each partner expresses to the other: being tender and considerate . . . so that deep, intimate communication occurs.

Creating times of romance is important. Try incorporating some of these ingredients into your personal romantic style.

- The element of the unexpected. Anything that is repeated month after month, year after year, can easily become humdrum.
- The element of dating. Laugh and enjoy each other and be a little crazy.
- The element of creativity. Discover what delights your partner and then make those delights happen in creative ways.
- The element of the daily romance involves daily acts of care, concern, love, listening and giving each other your personal attention.
- The element of commitment. If commitment to each other is at the heart of your marriage, romance will thrive.

H. Norman Wright

God's Words of Life on
SERVANTHOOD

Your attitude should be the same as that of Christ Jesus: Who, being in very nature God, did not consider equality with God something to be grasped, but made himself nothing, taking the very nature of a servant, being made in human likeness. And being found in appearance as a man, he humbled himself and became obedient to death—even death on a cross!

Philippians 2:5–8

The greatest among you will be your servant.

Matthew 23:11

Whoever wants to become great among you must be your servant, and whoever wants to be first must be slave of all.

Mark 10:43–44

The greatest among you should be like the youngest, and the one who rules like the one who serves. For who is greater, the one who is at the table or the one who serves? Is it not the one who is at the table? But I am among you as one who serves.

Luke 22:26–27

There are different kinds of service, but the same Lord.

1 Corinthians 12:5

I have set you an example that you should do
as I have done for you. I tell you the truth, no
servant is greater than his master, nor is a
messenger greater than the one who sent him.

John 13:15–16

Though I am free and belong to no man, I
make myself a slave to everyone, to win as
many as possible. To the Jews I became like a
Jew, to win the Jews. To those under the law I
became like one under the law (though I myself
am not under the law), so as to win those
under the law. To those not having the law I
became like one not having the law (though I
am not free from God's law but am under
Christ's law), so as to win those not having the
law. To the weak I became weak, to win the
weak. I have become all things to all men so
that by all possible means I might save some.

1 Corinthians 9:19–22

Jesus said to him, "For it is written: 'Worship
the Lord your God, and serve him only.'"

Matthew 4:10

Be very careful to keep the commandment. . .
that Moses the servant of the LORD gave to
you, to walk in all his ways, to obey his commands, to hold fast to him and to serve him
with all your heart and all your soul.

Joshua 22:5

God's Words of Life on
SERVANTHOOD

Whoever wants to save his life will lose it, but whoever loses his life for me will find it.

Matthew 16:25

Be devoted to one another in brotherly love. Honor one another above yourselves. Never be lacking in zeal, but keep your spiritual fervor, serving the Lord.

Romans 12:10–11

What does the LORD your God ask of you but to fear the LORD your God, to walk in all his ways, to love him, to serve the LORD your God with all your heart and with all your soul.

Deuteronomy 10:12–13

Serve wholeheartedly, as if you were serving the Lord, not men, because you know that the Lord will reward everyone for whatever good he does.

Ephesians 6:7

For even the Son of Man did not come to be served, but to serve, and to give his life as a ransom for many.

Mark 10:45

SERVANTHOOD

SECRET SERVANTHOOD

We spotted Mr. Per as we backed our van into campsite number seven. He was disappearing through the white birch and pine that separated our parking spot from his. "Somebody's raked our spot," my daughter Jori said. Later, we saw a rake leaning against a Winnebago.

When we returned from a walk, we found a pile of neatly stacked logs beside our fireplace, and two coloring books lay on the picnic table.

"Somebody likes kids," was all Mr. Per said next morning when I mentioned the coloring books. The next night our lantern was lit for us when we made our way up the path from the lake. He had hung it to light the rocky way we had to walk. Mr. Per was whistling through the woods, heading toward his site just as we walked into camp.

Our lives had been touched by a man who knew something profound about service. Mr. Per demonstrated for us what Jesus taught: "Do not let your left hand know what your right hand is doing, so that your giving may be in secret. Then your Father, who sees what is done in secret, will reward you" (Matthew 6:3–4).

Ruth Senter

God's Words of Life *on*
SPIRITUAL LIFE

Love the LORD your God with all your heart and with all your soul and with all your strength.

Deuteronomy 6:5

You will keep in perfect peace him whose mind is steadfast, because he trusts in you.

Isaiah 26:3

The kingdom of God is not a matter of eating and drinking, but of righteousness, peace and joy in the Holy Spirit.

Romans 14:17

You have been raised with Christ, set your hearts on things above, where Christ is seated at the right hand of God. Set your minds on things above, not on earthly things.

Colossians 3:1–2

Blessed are those who hunger and thirst for righteousness, for they will be filled.

Matthew 5:6

Do not work for food that spoils, but for food that endures to eternal life, which the Son of Man will give you.

John 6:27

I will ask the Father, and he will give you another Counselor to be with you forever— the Spirit of truth. The world cannot accept him, because it neither sees him nor knows him. But you know him, for he lives with you and will be in you.

John 14:16–17

This is what the LORD says: "Stand at the crossroads and look; ask for the ancient paths, ask where the good way is, and walk in it, and you will find rest for your souls."

Jeremiah 6:16

You desire truth in the inner parts; you teach me wisdom in the inmost place.

Psalm 51:6

Grow in the grace and knowledge of our Lord and Savior Jesus Christ. To him be glory both now and forever! Amen.

2 Peter 3:18

Being confident of this, that he who began a good work in you will carry it on to completion until the day of Christ Jesus . . . that your love may abound more and more in knowledge and depth of insight, so that you may be able to discern what is best and may be pure and blameless until the day of Christ.

Philippians 1:6,9–10

God's Words of Life on
SPIRITUAL LIFE

LORD, who may dwell in your sanctuary?
Who may live on your holy hill? He whose
walk is blameless and who does what is righteous, who speaks the truth from his heart.

Psalm 15:1–2

The fruit of righteousness will be peace; the
effect of righteousness will be quietness and
confidence forever.

Isaiah 32:17

Remain in me, and I will remain in you. No
branch can bear fruit by itself; it must remain
in the vine. Neither can you bear fruit unless
you remain in me. I am the vine; you are the
branches. If a man remains in me and I in
him, he will bear much fruit; apart from me
you can do nothing.

John 15:4–5

He follows my decrees and faithfully keeps
my laws. That man is righteous; he will surely live, declares the Sovereign LORD.

Ezekiel 18:9

He has showed you, O man, what is good.
And what does the LORD require of you? To
act justly and to love mercy and to walk
humbly with your God.

Micah 6:8

By this all men will know that you are my
disciples, if you love one another.

John 13:35

Jesus replied, "If anyone loves me, he will
obey my teaching. My Father will love him,
and we will come to him and make our home
with him.

John 14:23

The one who sows to please his sinful nature,
from that nature will reap destruction; the
one who sows to please the Spirit, from the
Spirit will reap eternal life. Let us not become
weary in doing good, for at the proper time
we will reap a harvest if we do not give up.

Galatians 6:8–9

One thing I do: Forgetting what is behind and
straining toward what is ahead, I press on
toward the goal to win the prize for which
God has called me heavenward in Christ Jesus.

Philippians 3:13–14

The grace of God that brings salvation has
appeared to all men. It teaches us to say
"No" to ungodliness and worldly passions,
and to live self-controlled, upright and godly
lives in this present age.

Titus 2:11–12

God's Words of Life *on*
SPIRITUAL LIFE

Everyone who hears these words of mine and puts them into practice is like a wise man who built his house on the rock. The rain came down, the streams rose, and the winds blew and beat against that house; yet it did not fall, because it had its foundation on the rock.

Matthew 7:24–25

SPIRITUAL LIFE

A GROWING LOVE

When one spouse is experiencing more rapid spiritual growth, there's a danger of putting pressure on the other partner: "She should say grace at meals" or "He should lead the family devotions."

Most people resist being told what to do! If one person is uncomfortable with something, then the spouse who is spiritually ready should go ahead to initiate and lead those activities. The point is not to nag, but to encourage one another. Encouraging literally means "putting the heart into people"—giving someone a heart or desire for something. A spouse may get encouraged as he or she sees the Holy Spirit work in their partner. That's a better way of encouraging each other than imposing your desires on your mate.

It all begins in being responsible for our own growing love for God. As we're absorbed in the Lord, it should be catching! It makes our partners hungry for that experience, but it does so without admonishing or pushing.

Jill and Stuart Briscoe

God's Words of Life *on*
STRESS

Come to me, all you who are weary and burdened, and I will give you rest. Take my yoke upon you and learn from me, for I am gentle and humble in heart, and you will find rest for your souls. For my yoke is easy and my burden is light.

Matthew 11:28–30

He gives strength to the weary and increases the power of the weak. Even youths grow tired and weary, and young men stumble and fall; but those who hope in the LORD will renew their strength. They will soar on wings like eagles; they will run and not grow weary, they will walk and not be faint.

Isaiah 40:29–31

Remember the Sabbath day by keeping it holy. Six days you shall labor and do all your work, but the seventh day is a Sabbath to the LORD your God. On it you shall not do any work, neither you, nor your son or daughter, nor your manservant or maidservant, nor your animals, nor the alien within your gates. For in six days the LORD made the heavens and the earth, the sea, and all that is in them, but he rested on the seventh day. Therefore the LORD blessed the Sabbath day and made it holy.

Exodus 20:8–11

Do not fear, for I am with you; do not be dismayed, for I am your God. I will strengthen you and help you; I will uphold you with my righteous right hand.

Isaiah 41:10

I will refresh the weary and satisfy the faint.

Jeremiah 31:25

Be strong in the Lord and in his mighty power.

Ephesians 6:10

Unless the LORD builds the house, its builders labor in vain. Unless the LORD watches over the city, the watchmen stand guard in vain. In vain you rise early and stay up late, toiling for food to eat—for he grants sleep to those he loves.

Psalm 127:1–2

Let us not become weary in doing good, for at the proper time we will reap a harvest if we do not give up.

Galatians 6:9

You are awesome, O God, in your sanctuary; the God of Israel gives power and strength to his people. Praise be to God!

Psalm 68:35

God's Words of Life on
STRESS

He makes me lie down in green pastures, he leads me beside quiet waters, he restores my soul. He guides me in paths of righteousness for his name's sake.

Psalm 23:2–3

Be at rest once more, O my soul,
 for the LORD has been good to you.

Psalm 116:7

He who dwells in the shelter of the Most High will rest in the shadow of the Almighty.

Psalm 91:1

Find rest, O my soul, in God alone; my hope comes from him.

Psalm 62:5

My soul finds rest in God alone; my salvation comes from him.

Psalm 62:1

Therefore my heart is glad and my tongue rejoices; my body also will rest secure.

Psalm 16:9

You will be secure, because there is hope; you will look about you and take your rest in safety.

Job 11:18

My soul is weary with sorrow; strengthen me according to your word.

Psalm 119:28

Let us fix our eyes on Jesus, the author and perfecter of our faith, who for the joy set before him endured the cross, scorning its shame, and sat down at the right hand of the throne of God. Consider him who endured such opposition from sinful men, so that you will not grow weary and lose heart.

Hebrews 12:2–3

Jesus said, "Peace I leave with you; my peace I give you. I do not give to you as the world gives. Do not let your hearts be troubled and do not be afraid."

John 14:27

For our struggle is not against flesh and blood, but against the rulers, against the authorities, against the powers of this dark world and against the spiritual forces of evil in the heavenly realms. Therefore put on the full armor of God, so that when the day of evil comes, you may be able to stand your ground, and after you have done everything, to stand.

Ephesians 6:12–13

God's Words of Life *on*
STRESS

Therefore I tell you, do not worry about your life, what you will eat or drink; or about your body, what you will wear. Is not life more important than food, and the body more important than clothes? Look at the birds of the air; they do not sow or reap or store away in barns, and yet your heavenly Father feeds them. Are you not much more valuable than they? Who of you by worrying can add a single hour to his life?

Matthew 6:25–27

By the seventh day God had finished the work he had been doing; so on the seventh day he rested from all his work.

Genesis 2:2

There remains, then, a Sabbath-rest for the people of God; for anyone who enters God's rest also rests from his own work, just as God did from his. Let us, therefore, make every effort to enter that rest, so that no one will fall by following their example of disobedience.

Hebrews 4:9–11

Jesus said to his disciples: "Come with me by yourselves to a quiet place and get some rest."

Mark 6:31

STRESS POINTS

Change points are stress points. My ten-
year-old loses his childhood innocence.
My skin takes on some wrinkles. And Mark,
my husband, leaves the pastorate to teach at a
seminary.

Sometimes change is a package I'd rather
return to the sender. I watch as a four-year-old
neighbor succumbs to leukemia's wasteland. I
watch as a friend's marriage turns sour. And I
grieve over the change.

In my quest for stability, I remember Job,
caught in chaotic upheavals—currents of
change that blew hard against all that he had
and was. I'm sure Job didn't glibly sing his
way from gentleman farmer to the ash heap.
In fact, he probably muttered under his breath
all the way. But when all his muttering was
done, he came face-to-face with his changeless
God. "My ears had heard of you but now my
eyes have seen you" (Job 42:5).

The changes in Job's life moved him toward
God. Stress points? Yes, but also opportunities
to discover new dimensions of God.

Ruth Senter

God's Words of Life *on*
SUFFERING

He was despised and rejected by men, a man of sorrows, and familiar with suffering. Like one from whom men hide their faces he was despised, and we esteemed him not.

Isaiah 53:3

Just as the sufferings of Christ flow over into our lives, so also through Christ our comfort overflows.

2 Corinthians 1:5

I consider that our present sufferings are not worth comparing with the glory that will be revealed in us.

Romans 8:18

For Christ's sake, I delight in weaknesses, in insults, in hardships, in persecutions, in difficulties. For when I am weak, then I am strong.

2 Corinthians 12:10

It has been granted to you on behalf of Christ not only to believe on him, but also to suffer for him.

Philippians 1:29

A righteous man may have many troubles, but the LORD delivers him from them all.

Psalm 34:19

Blessed is the man who perseveres under trial, because when he has stood the test, he will receive the crown of life that God has promised to those who love him.

James 1:12

He knows the way that I take; when he has tested me, I will come forth as gold.

Job 23:10

If you are insulted because of the name of Christ, you are blessed, for the Spirit of glory and of God rests on you.

1 Peter 4:14

No discipline seems pleasant at the time, but painful. Later on, however, it produces a harvest of righteousness and peace for those who have been trained by it.

Hebrews 12:11

Everyone who wants to live a godly life in Christ Jesus will be persecuted.

2 Timothy 3:12

Blessed is the man whom God corrects; so do not despise the discipline of the Almighty. For he wounds, but he also binds up; he injures, but his hands also heal.

Job 5:17–18

God's Words of Life *on*
SUFFERING

We also rejoice in our sufferings, because we know that suffering produces perseverance; perseverance, character; and character, hope.

Romans 5:3–4

Endure hardship with us like a good soldier of Christ Jesus.

2 Timothy 2:3

Because he himself suffered when he was tempted, he is able to help those who are being tempted.

Hebrews 2:18

The LORD disciplines those he loves, as a father the son he delights in.

Proverbs 3:12

The LORD said, "I have indeed seen the misery of my people . . . and I am concerned about their suffering.

Exodus 3:7

Those who suffer he delivers in their suffering; he speaks to them in their affliction.

Job 36:15

My comfort in my suffering is this: Your promise preserves my life.

Psalm 119:50

After the suffering of his soul, he will see the light of life and be satisfied.

Isaiah 53:11

When Jesus had entered Capernaum, a centurion came to him, asking for help. "Lord," he said, "my servant lies at home paralyzed and in terrible suffering." Jesus said to him, "I will go and heal him."

Matthew 8:5–7

Consider it pure joy, my brothers, whenever you face trials of many kinds, because you know that the testing of your faith develops perseverance.

James 1:2–3

He has not despised or disdained the suffering of the afflicted one; he has not hidden his face from him but has listened to his cry for help.

Psalm 22:24

Cast your cares on the LORD and he will sustain you; he will never let the righteous fall.

Psalm 55:22

Those who sow in tears will reap with songs of joy. He who goes out weeping, carrying seed to sow, will return with songs of joy, carrying sheaves with him.

Psalm 126:5–6

God's Words of Life *on*
SUFFERING

In bringing many sons to glory, it was fitting
that God, for whom and through whom
everything exists, should make the author of
their salvation perfect through suffering.

Hebrews 2:10

Brothers, as an example of patience in the
face of suffering, take the prophets who
spoke in the name of the Lord. As you know,
we consider blessed those who have perse-
vered. You have heard of Job's perseverance
and have seen what the Lord finally brought
about. The Lord is full of compassion and
mercy.

James 5:10–11

If you suffer for doing good and you endure
it, this is commendable before God. To this
you were called, because Christ suffered for
you, leaving you an example, that you
should follow in his steps.

1 Peter 2:20–21

Dear friends, do not be surprised at the
painful trial you are suffering, as though
something strange were happening to you.
But rejoice that you participate in the sufferings of Christ, so that you may be overjoyed
when his glory is revealed.

1 Peter 4:12–13

THE PRUNING OF SUFFERING

A peach tree stands in our back yard. Unpruned, the tree grew big and leafy. The year my husband, Larry, was out of work, he went to work on the tree. When I came home from school one day and saw how far back he had pruned it, I stared in shock. "You've killed it," I cried. "Now we won't have any peaches at all."

But I was wrong. That spring the pruned branches burst forth with a beautiful blanketing of pink blossoms. Soon little green peaches replaced the blossoms. "Leave them alone," I begged. Larry ignored me and thinned the fruit.

By the end of summer the branches were so heavily laden with fruit they had to be propped up. There was no denying it: The tree was far better off for the painful cutting it endured under Larry's pruning shears.

No one wants to go through troubles and suffering and pain. It was eleven months before Larry got a job. Looking back, we can only say, "Thank you, Lord, for pruning us. Thank you for teaching us to trust you. Thank you for drawing us together as a family and welding us in a way that never happened in happier times. Thank you, that after seeing each other at our worst, we still want to be together."

Kay Marshall Strom

God's Words of Life on
THANKFULNESS

Give thanks to the LORD, for he is good; his love endures forever. Let the redeemed of the LORD say this.

Psalm 107:1–2

I will extol the LORD at all times; his praise will always be on my lips.

Psalm 34:1

Let the peace of Christ rule in your hearts, since as members of one body you were called to peace. And be thankful. Let the word of Christ dwell in you richly as you teach and admonish one another with all wisdom, and as you sing psalms, hymns and spiritual songs with gratitude in your hearts to God. And whatever you do, whether in word or deed, do it all in the name of the Lord Jesus, giving thanks to God the Father through him.

Colossians 3:15–17

Give thanks in all circumstances, for this is God's will for you in Christ Jesus.

1 Thessalonians 5:18

Thanks be to God! He gives us the victory through our Lord Jesus Christ.

1 Corinthians 15:57

THANKFULNESS

Give thanks to the LORD, call on his name;
make known among the nations what he has
done.

1 Chronicles 16:8

Praise the LORD. I will extol the LORD with all
my heart in the council of the upright and in
the assembly. Great are the works of the
LORD; they are pondered by all who delight
in them.

Psalm 111:1–2

Thanks be to God for his indescribable gift!

2 Corinthians 9:15

Always giving thanks to God the Father for
everything, in the name of our Lord Jesus
Christ.

Ephesians 5:20

Rooted and built up in him, strengthened in
the faith as you were taught, and overflow-
ing with thankfulness.

Colossians 2:7

Sing to the LORD with thanksgiving; make
music to our God on the harp.

Psalm 147:7

God's Words of Life on
THANKFULNESS

Enter his gates with thanksgiving and his courts with praise; give thanks to him and praise his name.

Psalm 100:4

I will sacrifice a thank offering to you and call on the name of the LORD.

Psalm 116:17

Everything God created is good, and nothing is to be rejected if it is received with thanksgiving.

1 Timothy 4:4

Through Jesus, therefore, let us continually offer to God a sacrifice of praise—the fruit of lips that confess his name.

Hebrews 13:15

RENEWED THROUGH THANKFULNESS

Following years of fruitful ministry, a pastor found himself beginning each new day with dread. Finally, the quagmire was so deep that he gave up his church and retreated to his home.

One day a former parishioner brought over a basket of fruit, and the pastor's wife asked her husband if he would write a note in response to the kindness. With considerable effort, the despondent pastor took up his pen and began writing. A trickle of warmth returned to his spirit as he wrote in praise of fruit baskets, and in praise of his former parishioner. Before the day was over, he had written also in praise of a deacon, a head usher and an organist who had never missed a Sunday in fifteen years.

His days now began to take on definition. One by one, he wrote in praise of the people in his life. Sometimes his words were blurred by his tears, but he wrote on until he once again greeted his day with zest, and closed it in praise. He had moved outside himself, and life had been renewed. The pastor returned to his little village church, a whole man, restored by the spirit of thankfulness.

Ruth Senter

God's Words of Life on
TIME

Teach us to number our days aright, that we may gain a heart of wisdom.

Psalm 90:12

Show me, O LORD, my life's end and the number of my days; let me know how fleeting is my life. You have made my days a mere handbreadth; the span of my years is as nothing before you. Each man's life is but a breath. Selah. Man is a mere phantom as he goes to and fro: He bustles about, but only in vain; he heaps up wealth, not knowing who will get it. But now, Lord, what do I look for? My hope is in you.

Psalm 39:4–7

Do not boast about tomorrow, for you do not know what a day may bring forth.

Proverbs 27:1

What is your life? You are a mist that appears for a little while and then vanishes. Instead, you ought to say, "If it is the Lord's will, we will live and do this or that."

James 4:14–15

Let everyone who is godly pray to you while you may be found; surely when the mighty waters rise, they will not reach him.

Psalm 32:6

Seek the LORD while he may be found; call on him while he is near. Let the wicked forsake his way and the evil man his thoughts. Let him turn to the LORD, and he will have mercy on him, and to our God, for he will freely pardon.

Isaiah 55:6–7

The hour has come for you to wake up from your slumber, because our salvation is nearer now than when we first believed. The night is nearly over; the day is almost here. So let us put aside the deeds of darkness and put on the armor of light.

Romans 13:11–12

Be patient, then, brothers, until the Lord's coming. See how the farmer waits for the land to yield its valuable crop and how patient he is for the autumn and spring rains. You too, be patient and stand firm, because the Lord's coming is near.

James 5:7–9

Make the most of every opportunity.

Colossians 4:5

As we have opportunity, let us do good to all people, especially to those who belong to the family of believers.

Galatians 6:10

God's Words of Life on
TIME

The time is short. From now on those who
have wives should live as if they had none;
those who mourn, as if they did not; those
who are happy, as if they were not; those
who buy something, as if it were not theirs to
keep; those who use the things of the world,
as if not engrossed in them. For this world in
its present form is passing away.

1 Corinthians 7:29–31

Jesus said: "The ground of a certain rich man
produced a good crop. He thought to himself, 'What shall I do? I have no place to store
my crops.' Then he said, 'This is what I'll do.
I will tear down my barns and build bigger
ones, and there I will store all my grain and
my goods. And I'll say to myself, "You have
plenty of good things laid up for many years.
Take life easy; eat, drink and be merry."' But
God said to him, 'You fool! This very night
your life will be demanded from you. Then
who will get what you have prepared for
yourself?' This is how it will be with anyone
who stores up things for himself but is not
rich toward God."

Luke 12:16–21

MAKING TIME FOR EACH OTHER

Spending time with God is the time to listen to the most important voice in heaven. Likewise, freeing up time with my wife is a time to listen to the most important voice on earth. My marriage commitment implies putting Karen first, and that's almost impossible to do if she cannot get on my agenda regularly.

If Karen feels unheard, she will eventually feel unloved. And that is a dangerous state. The Bible warns "Under three things the earth trembles, under four it cannot bear up: ... an unloved woman who is married" (Proverbs 30:21,23).

Karen will not feel loved if I don't spend time with her. She craves a oneness that can only be built through daily debriefings. But as delays go from days to weeks, the postponed agendas pile up and the volcano starts to rumble. Finally, a conversation starts out slowly, then it picks up momentum, knocking loose a score of larger thoughts. Every item she shares with me reminds her of another. Before long, I'm buried in an avalanche! I ask her, "Why did you wait so long to tell me all this?"

She doesn't need to answer. She tried, but I was traveling too fast to hear, or I didn't leave any time in which she could even try.

Ron Hutchcraft

God's Words of Life *on*
TRUST

Those who know your name will trust in you, for you, LORD, have never forsaken those who seek you.

Psalm 9:10

Blessed is the man who trusts in the LORD, whose confidence is in him. He will be like a tree planted by the water that sends out its roots by the stream. It does not fear when heat comes; its leaves are always green. It has no worries in a year of drought and never fails to bear fruit.

Jeremiah 17:7–8

[Abraham] did not waver through unbelief regarding the promise of God, but was strengthened in his faith and gave glory to God, being fully persuaded that God had power to do what he had promised.

Romans 4:20–21

Taste and see that the LORD is good; blessed is the man who takes refuge in him.

Psalm 34:8

O LORD Almighty, blessed is the man who trusts in you.

Psalm 84:12

Those who trust in the LORD are like Mount Zion, which cannot be shaken but endures forever.

Psalm 125:1

Whoever gives heed to instruction prospers, and blessed is he who trusts in the LORD.

Proverbs 16:20

You will keep in perfect peace him whose mind is steadfast, because he trusts in you. Trust in the LORD forever, for the LORD, the LORD, is the Rock eternal.

Isaiah 26:3–4

The LORD longs to be gracious to you; he rises to show you compassion. For the LORD is a God of justice. Blessed are all who wait for him!

Isaiah 30:18

Many are the woes of the wicked, but the LORD's unfailing love surrounds the man who trusts in him.

Psalm 32:10

Trust in the LORD and do good; dwell in the land and enjoy safe pasture.

Psalm 37:3

God's Words of Life *on*
TRUST

Blessed is the man who makes the LORD his trust, who does not look to the proud, to those who turn aside to false gods.

Psalm 40:4

Trust in the LORD with all your heart and lean not on your own understanding.

Proverbs 3:5

He who trusts in the LORD will prosper.

Proverbs 28:25

Be strong and take heart, all you who hope in the LORD.

Psalm 31:24

Fear of man will prove to be a snare, but whoever trusts in the LORD is kept safe.

Proverbs 29:25

The LORD is good, a refuge in times of trouble. He cares for those who trust in him.

Nahum 1:7

IT TAKES TWO TO TRUST

In marriage, it takes two to trust. When I decided to leave a secure job so I could stay home and write full-time, my husband, Fritz, encouraged the move. Since then, we've learned over and over the meaning of my favorite proverb: "Trust in the LORD with all your heart and lean not on your own understanding; in all your ways acknowledge him, and he will make your paths straight" (Proverbs 3:5–6).

God demands that we rely totally on him; anything less is disobedience. No concern is too small, no issue too complex to bring to him.

That may be why Fritz and I, through the ups and downs of our life, have felt fundamentally confident about the future. We have tried to rise above the good news/bad news syndrome; that is, feeling great when things go well and despairing when they don't. Those emotions come and go. God's peace, which settles deep inside you, won't.

And it's available to every one of us who trusts in him—wholly.

Elizabeth Cody Newenhuyse

God's Words of Life on
WISDOM

Get wisdom, get understanding; do not forget my words or swerve from them. Do not forsake wisdom, and she will protect you; love her, and she will watch over you. Wisdom is supreme; therefore get wisdom. Though it cost all you have, get understanding.

Proverbs 4:5–7

The fear of the Lord—that is wisdom, and to shun evil is understanding.

Job 28:28

I will instruct you and teach you in the way you should go; I will counsel you and watch over you.

Psalm 32:8

I guide you in the way of wisdom and lead you along straight paths. When you walk, your steps will not be hampered; when you run, you will not stumble.

Proverbs 4:11–12

Trust in the LORD with all your heart and lean not on your own understanding; in all your ways acknowledge him, and he will make your paths straight.

Proverbs 3:5–7

Whether you turn to the right or to the left, your ears will hear a voice behind you, saying, "This is the way; walk in it."

Isaiah 30:21

The wisdom that comes from heaven is first of all pure; then peace-loving, considerate, submissive, full of mercy and good fruit, impartial and sincere.

James 3:17

My son, if you accept my words and store up my commands within you, turning your ear to wisdom and applying your heart to understanding, and if you call out for insight and cry aloud for understanding, and if you look for it as for silver and search for it as for hidden treasure, then you will understand the fear of the LORD and find the knowledge of God. For the LORD gives wisdom, and from his mouth come knowledge and understanding.

Proverbs 2:1–6

Where then does wisdom come from? Where does understanding dwell? It is hidden from the eyes of every living thing, concealed even from the birds of the air... God understands the way to it and he alone knows where it dwells.

Job 28:20–21,23

God's Words of Life on
WISDOM

The foolishness of God is wiser than man's wisdom, and the weakness of God is stronger than man's strength.

1 Corinthians 1:25

Pay attention to my wisdom, listen well to my words of insight, that you may maintain discretion and your lips may preserve knowledge.

Proverbs 5:1–2

Your commands make me wiser than my enemies, for they are ever with me.

Psalm 119:98

Whoever listens to me will live in safety and be at ease, without fear of harm.

Proverbs 1:33

If any of you lacks wisdom, he should ask God, who gives generously to all without finding fault, and it will be given to him.

James 1:5

SEEK DISCERNMENT

If you could have anything in the world simply by asking, what would you request? Perfect health? The ideal job?

That question might make for pleasant after-dinner conversation, but it happened to King Solomon. God appeared to him in a dream, asking him to name whatever it was that he desired. Solomon could have asked for victory over his enemies, a cooperative citizenry, personal riches. But instead, he asked for "a discerning heart" to govern God's people and to "distinguish between right and wrong" (1 Kings 3:9). Solomon was asking for the tools he would need to do his job well.

If God were to ask you what you desire most for your marriage, what would you say? An end to your disagreements? The ability to get out of debt? Those are end results. Perhaps God wants us to focus instead on the qualities each of us needs in order to achieve the results he desires. A good place to start is by seeking discernment.

Solomon sought the ability to distinguish between right and wrong so he could employ that wisdom in his dealings with the people of Israel. In our marriages, we need that same discernment in our dealings with each other. The success of our marriages depends on it.

Ron and Jeanette Lee

God's Words of Life *on*
WORK

Whatever your hand finds to do, do it with all your might.

Ecclesiastes 9:10

Lazy hands make a man poor, but diligent hands bring wealth.

Proverbs 10:4

Six days you shall labor and do all your work, but the seventh day is a Sabbath to the LORD your God.

Deuteronomy 5:13

He who gathers money little by little makes it grow.

Proverbs 13:11

All hard work brings a profit.

Proverbs 14:23

Jesus said: "The harvest is plentiful, but the workers are few. Ask the Lord of the harvest, therefore, to send out workers into his harvest field."

Luke 10:2

My heart took delight in all my work, and this was the reward for all my labor.

Ecclesiastes 2:10

The plans of the diligent lead to profit as
surely as haste leads to poverty.

Proverbs 21:5

There are different kinds of gifts, but the
same Spirit. There are different kinds of service, but the same Lord. There are different
kinds of working, but the same God works
all of them in all men.

1 Corinthians 12:4–6

Make it your ambition to lead a quiet life, to
mind your own business and to work with
your hands, just as we told you, so that your
daily life may win the respect of outsiders
and so that you will not be dependent on
anybody.

1 Thessalonians 4:11–12

Two are better than one, because they have a
good return for their work.

Ecclesiastes 4:9

I planted the seed, Apollos watered it, but
God made it grow. So neither he who plants
nor he who waters is anything, but only God,
who makes things grow. The man who plants
and the man who waters have one purpose,
and each will be rewarded according to his
own labor.

1 Corinthians 3:6–8

God's Words of Life *on*
WORK

The LORD your God will bless you in all your harvest and in all the work of your hands, and your joy will be complete.

Deuteronomy 16:15

Do you see a man skilled in his work? He will serve before kings.

Proverbs 22:29

Carry each other's burdens, and in this way you will fulfill the law of Christ.

Galatians 6:2

Well done, good and faithful servant! You have been faithful with a few things; I will put you in charge of many things. Come and share your master's happiness!

Matthew 25:21

WORK ON YOUR RELATIONSHIP TOO

How can you keep job stress from having a negative effect on your marriage?

First, don't let your marriage become a dumping ground for your work frustrations. If the only conversation that takes place between a husband and wife is about work, the marriage will eventually burn out. Intimacy can't grow between two people who never explore any of the deeper issues in their lives.

Second, especially with dual-career couples, guard against emotional detachment. Each spouse gets wrapped up in his or her own career, and work becomes a gauge of their self-esteem, rather than the two of them nurturing each other.

In contrast, if a couple develops a habit of showing appreciation for the things they value in each other, it will help each of them see his or her value apart from their work. You have to practice affirming your partner before it will become second nature to you. Too many spouses say, "Oh, she knows I like that about her," or, "He knows I value that quality in him." No, they don't know. You need to tell your partner these things over and over.

Archibald D. Hart, Ph.D.

God's Words of Life on
WORRY

Cast your cares on the LORD and he will sustain you; he will never let the righteous fall.

Psalm 55:22

Commit your way to the LORD; trust in him and he will do this: He will make your righteousness shine like the dawn, the justice of your cause like the noonday sun.

Psalm 37:5–6

Look at the birds of the air; they do not sow or reap or store away in barns, and yet your heavenly Father feeds them. Are you not much more valuable than they?

Matthew 6:26

Who of you by worrying can add a single hour to his life?

Matthew 6:27

Cast all your anxiety on him because he cares for you.

1 Peter 5:7

Jesus said to his disciples: "Therefore I tell you, do not worry about your life, what you will eat; or about your body, what you will wear. Life is more than food, and the body more than clothes."

Luke 12:22–23

Do not worry about tomorrow, for tomorrow will worry about itself. Each day has enough trouble of its own.

Matthew 6:34

The LORD himself goes before you and will be with you; he will never leave you nor forsake you. Do not be afraid; do not be discouraged.

Deuteronomy 31:8

Do not be anxious about anything, but in everything, by prayer and petition, with thanksgiving, present your requests to God. And the peace of God, which transcends all understanding, will guard your hearts and your minds in Christ Jesus.

Philippians 4:6–7

Be strong and very courageous. Be careful to obey all the law my servant Moses gave you; do not turn from it to the right or to the left, that you may be successful wherever you go.

Joshua 1:7

God did not give us a spirit of timidity, but a spirit of power, of love and of self-discipline.

2 Timothy 1:7

He who fears the LORD has a secure fortress, and for his children it will be a refuge.

Proverbs 14:26

God's Words of Life on
WORRY

We say with confidence, "The LORD is my helper; I will not be afraid. What can man do to me?"

Hebrews 13:6

The LORD is with you when you are with him. If you seek him, he will be found by you.

2 Chronicles 15:2

Do not be afraid, little flock, for your Father has been pleased to give you the kingdom.

Luke 12:32

When you lie down, you will not be afraid; when you lie down, your sleep will be sweet.

Proverbs 3:24

STRENGTH INSTEAD OF WORRY

It was a familiar story. The Israelites had been flagrantly disobedient, and now they were under fire from one of their many enemies, the Midianites. In times like these, God would call forth a judge to lead his people back to righteous living and back into political peace.

Isn't it just like God to choose a person like Gideon, a regular, everyday kind of guy with a real self-confidence problem? When Gideon expressed his doubts, God commented, "Go in the strength you have... Am I not sending you?" (Judges 6:14) and promised, "I will be with you" (6:16). Gideon still had doubts, and God was patient with him while Gideon gained the confidence to obey his Lord.

Everybody feels inadequate sometimes—as an employee on the job, as a spouse, as a parent, as a Christian seeking to obey God. God's answer to our insecurities is "Go in the strength you have... I will be with you."

Annette's mom used to have a plaque on her kitchen wall that read, "The will of God will never lead you where the grace of God cannot keep you." We can tackle the responsibilities God has placed before us, while we hang onto that promise.

David and Annette LaPlaca

SOURCES

David and Claudia Arp, *The Marriage Track*, © 1992 by David and Claudia Arp. Thomas Nelson Publishers, Nashville, Tennessee.

Steve Arterburn, *Addicted to Love*, © 1992 by Stephen Arterburn. Servant Publications, Ann Arbor, MI.

Stuart and Jill Briscoe, Taken from an interview with Jill and Stuart Briscoe, by Annette LaPlaca, that originally appeared in the Fall 1993 issue of *Marriage Partnership* magazine. © 1993 by Christianity Today, Inc.

Evelyn Christenson, Taken from an interview with Evelyn Christenson, by Phyllis E. Alsdurf, that originally appeared in the March/April 1985 issue of *Partnership* magazine. © 1985 by Phyllis E. Alsdurf.

Jim Conway, Taken from an interview with Jim and Sally Conway, by Ron R. Lee, that originally appeared in the Winter 1993 issue of *Marriage Partnership* magazine. © 1993 by Christianity Today, Inc.

Lyn Cryderman, Taken from an article by Lyn Cryderman that originally appeared in the Spring 1992 issue of *Marriage Partnership* magazine. © 1992 by Lyn Cryderman.

Preston and Genie Dyer, Taken from an article by Preston and Genie Dyer that originally appeared in the Fall 1992 issue of *Marriage Partnership* magazine. © 1992 by Preston and Genie Dyer.

Diane Eble, Taken from an article by Diane Eble that originally appeared in the Spring 1992 issue of *Marriage Partnership* magazine. © 1992 by Diane Eble.

Lowell and Carol Erdahl, *Be Good to Each Other*, 1991, Augsburg Fortress: Minneapolis.

Hope Harley, Taken from an article by Hope Harley that originally appeared in the Spring 1992 issue of *Marriage Partnership* magazine. © 1992 by Hope Harley.

Archibald D. Hart, Ph.D., Taken from an article by Archibald D. Hart, Ph.D., that originally appeared in the Fall 1991 issue of *Marriage Partnership* magazine. © 1991 by Archibald D. Hart, Ph.D.

SOURCES

Jeanne Hendricks, Taken from an interview with Jeanne Hendricks, by Ruth Senter, that originally appeared in the May/June 1985 issue of *Partnership* magazine. © 1985 by Christianity Today, Inc.

Ron Hutchcraft, *Peaceful Living in a Stressful World*, © 1984 by Ron Hutchcraft. Thomas Nelson: Nashville, TN.

Bill Hybels, *Honest to God*, © 1990 by Bill Hybels, Zondervan: Grand Rapids, MI.

David and Annette LaPlaca, Written by David and Annette LaPlaca. © 1994 by Christianity Today, Inc. Used by permission.

Drs. Robert and Jeanette Lauer, Taken from an article by Jeanette and Robert Lauer that originally appeared in the Fall 1992 issue of *Marriage Partnership* magazine. © 1992 by Jeanette and Robert Lauer.

Ron and Jeanette Lee, Written by Ron and Jeanette Lee. © 1994 by Christianity Today, Inc. Used by permission.

Marian V. Liautaud, Taken from an article by Susan M. Bailey that originally appeared in the Spring 1991 issue of *Marriage Partnership* magazine. Copyright © 1991 by Christianity Today, Inc. Used by permission.

Donna B. Lobs, Taken from an article by Donna Lobs that originally appeared in the January/February 1984 issue of *Partnership* magazine. © 1984 by Donna Lobs.

Dawson McAllister, Taken from an interview with Dawson McAllister, by Ron R. Lee, that originally appeared in the Summer 1993 issue of *Marriage Partnership* magazine. © 1993 by Christianity Today, Inc.

Louis McBurney, M.D., Taken from an article by Louis McBurney, M.D., that originally appeared in the Winter 1993 issue of *Marriage Partnership* magazine. © 1993 by Louis McBurney, M.D.

Elizabeth C. Newenhuyse, Taken from an article by Elizabeth Cody Newenhuyse that originally appeared in the Spring 1992 issue of *Marriage Partnership* magazine. Copyright © 1992 by Christianity Today, Inc. Used by permission. Also taken from *Strong Marriages, Secret*

SOURCES

Questions, © 1990 by Elizabeth Cody Newenhuyse. Lion Publishers/David C. Cook Publishing Company: Colorado Springs.

Ruth Senter, Taken from articles by Ruth Senter that originally appeared in the May/June 1985 issue, the March/April1986 issue and the July/August 1986 issue of *Partnership* magazine. © 1986 by Christianity Today, Inc. Used by permission.

Dr. Lewis Smedes, Taken from an interview with Lewis B. Smedes, by James D. Berkley, that originally appeared in the Winter 1991 issue of *Marriage Partnership* magazine. © 1991 by James D. Berkley.

Kay Marshall Strom, Taken from an article by Kay Marshall Strom that originally appeared in the Spring 1988 issue of *Marriage Partnership* magazine. © 1988 by Kay Marshall Strom.

Charles Swindoll, *Strike the Original Match*, 1993, Zondervan: Grand Rapids, MI.

Joni Eareckson Tada, Taken from an article by Joni Eareckson Tada that originally appeared in the January/February 1988 issue of *Marriage Partnership* magazine. © 1988 by Joni Eareckson Tada.

Alesia T. Thayer, Taken from an article by Alesia T. Thayer that originally appeared in the September/October 1984 issue of *Partnership* magazine. © 1984 by Alesia T. Thayer.

Charlie Wedemeyer, *Charlie's Victory*, © 1993 by Charlie and Lucy Wedemeyer, Zondervan: Grand Rapids, MI.

H. Norman Wright, *Making Peace with Your Partner*, © 1988 by H. Norman Wright, Word, Inc: Dallas. Holding on to Romance, © 1987, 1992 by Regal Books, a division of Gospel Light, Ventura, CA.

Susan Alexander Yates, *Marriage: Questions Women Ask*, © 1992 by Christianity Today, Inc., Questar Publishers/Multnomah Books: Sisters, QR.